Time Line Therapy
and
The Basis of Personality

Time Line Therapy
and
The Basis of Personality

By Tad James
and Wyatt Woodsmall

Meta Publications Inc.
P. 0. Box 1910, Capitola, CA 95010
(408) 464-0254 Fax (408) 464-0517

Library of Congress Card Number 87-063197
I.S.B.N. 0-916990-21-4

Table Of Contents

To Milton Erickson
Who Knew This Long Before We Did,

To Richard Bandler
Who Showed Us Where It Was

To Ardie James, and Eileen James
For Their Assistance In Editing
And For Their Support.

Acknowledgements

I would like to personally acknowledge all my teachers. Some of whom I met, and some of whom I have not met. The most important include Maharishi Mahesh Yogi, Swami Muktananda, John Garner, Leonard Orr, Werner Erhard, Stuart Novick, Trinidad Hunt, Dana Hall, Milton Erickson, Ernest Rossi, Richard Bandler, John Grinder, Steve Andreas, Wyatt Woodsmall, Robert Klaus, Cathy Modrall, Robert Dilts, Tony Robbins, Richard Roop, and of course all my students who have taught me as much.

These people are responsible for who I am today. They gave me the information. Of course, I accepted it, so I bear at least an equivalent responsibility. I thank them all for their part.

WARNING: The techniques described in this book are extremely powerful, and have the possibility of changing a person's personality totally and completely in a very short period of time. It is therefore important, for your safety and the safety of your client, that any therapeutic use of these techniques be done by someone trained in Time Line Therapy™. For training in Time Line Therapy in your area, contact: Tad James, ProfitAbility Group, Inc., P. O. Box 3768, Honolulu, HI 96812.

I

Introduction

Introduction

We are at the beginning of a new era of understanding. Over time, as we worked with a number of clients, it became obvious that we had discovered elements that make up a person's personality. We tested and found that, as we used this model for change, we were able to create seemingly miraculous changes in individuals, and at the deepest level of personality.

Models are interesting devices. They are descriptions or simulations of how something works in a certain area. In essence a model is a blueprint or a map. Like a map, a model is not necessarily "true." It is just a representation of reality. So we are not necessarily looking for truth in making this model; we are only attempting to describe how the human personality works. Like a map, it is only a description; and the value of any map or blueprint is in the result that you can produce by using it.

Our model seems to be a major discovery. This is a discovery for which psychologists from Freud and Jung to Isabel Briggs Myers have been searching. This model has the potential to change human understanding for all time to come, for we now understand and can change the basic elements that make up a person's personality. We now know the basis of personality and how to change it.

The model that we are calling the Basis of Personality is based on another earlier model, which is one of how we communicate with ourselves and with others. This model, which is essentially a model from Cognitive Psychology, was developed by Richard Bandler and John Grinder. It is called Neuro Linguistic Programming (NLP), and it explains how we process the information that comes into us from the world around us.

As we look at the NLP model, the process begins with an external event that we experience through our senses. Our

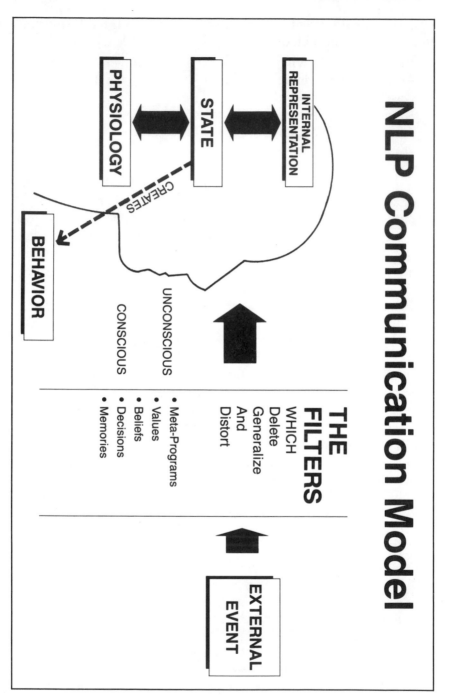

cognition of the event occurs as we experience the information that comes in through our sensory input channels which are:

Visual including what we see or the way someone looks at us;
Auditory which includes sounds, the words we hear and the way that people say those words to us;
Kinesthetic or external feelings, which include the touch of someone or something, the pressure and the texture;
Olfactory which is smell; and
Gustatory which is taste.

After the external event comes in through our sensory input channels, and before we make an Internal Representation (IR) of the event, we filter the event. We run that event through our internal processing filters. Our internal processing filters are how we delete, distort and generalize the information that comes in through our five senses.

DELETION

Deletion occurs when we selectively pay attention to certain aspects of our experience and not others. Deletion means we overlook or omit certain sensory information. Without deletion, we would be faced with much too much information to handle in our conscious minds.

DISTORTION

Distortion occurs when we make shifts in our experience of sensory data by making misrepresentations of reality. There's a well known story of distortion in Eastern philosophy. It is called the story of the rope and the snake. A man walking along a road saw what he believed to be a snake and yelled, "SNAKE." However, upon closer investigation he is relieved to discover that it really was only a piece of rope.

Distortion also helps us in the process of motivating ourselves. Motivation occurs when we actually distort the material that has come to us and that has already been changed by one of our filtering systems. Distortion is also helpful in planning. We distort to plan when we construct imaginary futures.

GENERALIZATION

The third process is generalization, where we draw global conclusions based on one, two or more experiences. At its best, generalization is one of the ways that we learn, whereby we take the information we have and draw broad conclusions about the world based on one or more experiences. At its worst, generalization is how we take a single event and make it into a lifetime of experience.

Normally the conscious mind can only handle seven, plus or minus two, items of information at any given time. Of course, many people cannot even handle this number. And I know people who have trouble with "one, plus or minus two"—the kind of people who cannot walk and chew gum. How about you? Try this: Can you name more than seven products in a given product category: for example, cigarettes? Most people will be able to name two, maybe three products in a category of low interest, and usually no more than nine in a category of high interest. There is a reason for this. If we did not actively delete information all the time, we would end up with excessive amounts of information coming in. In fact, you may have even heard that psychologists say that if we were simultaneously aware of all of the sensory information that was coming in, we would go crazy. That is why we filter the information.

So the question is, "When two people have the same stimulus, why don't they have the same response?" The answer is: because we delete, distort, and generalize the information from the outside in different ways.*

We delete, distort and generalize the information that comes in from our senses by using certain internal processing filters. The filters are: Meta Programs, Values, Beliefs, Attitudes, Decisions and Memories.

META PROGRAMS

Meta Programs are the most unconscious of the internal processing filters, and they are content-free filters. That is to say that Meta Programs in and of themselves have no content, but they do filter the content of our experience. Meta Programs are

---

*For ways of recognizing deletions, distortions and generalizations, and restoring them, see *Structure of Magic I*, Bandler, R.; et al.; 1975 Meta Publications

deletion and distortion filters that either add to or subtract from our generalizations. Meta Programs are just one of the ways we maintain our identities by either preserving or breaking down the generalizations that we make over time. Since knowing someone's Meta Programs can actually help you closely predict his states, they can be used to predict behavior—their actions. In addition, we can change the ways a person filters information for a certain purpose. The purpose of Meta Programs is NOT to put people into boxes (which we resist), or for the purpose of determining right or wrong. Meta Programs are not good or bad. They are simply one way a person processes information.

VALUES

The next most unconscious filter is our values. Values are the first level where the filters have content in and of themselves and are essentially an evaluation filter. They are how we decide whether our actions are good or bad or right or wrong. Values are how we decide about how we feel about our actions, and they provide the primary motivating force behind our actions. Values are arranged in a hierarchy, with the most important one typically being at the top and lesser ones below that. Each of us has varying models of the world (an internal representation of how the world is), and our values are interrelated with our models of the world. When we communicate with ourselves or someone else, if our model of the world conflicts with our values or their values, there is likely to be a conflict. Richard Bandler says, "Values are those things we don't live up to." Values are those ideas in which we are willing to invest time, energy and resources to either achieve or avoid.

Values are what people typically move toward or away from (see Meta Programs). They are our attractions or repulsions in life. They are generalizations about deep belief systems, which can be either unconscious or conscious, about what is important and what we evaluate as good or bad. Values can change with context. That is, you probably have certain values about what you want in a relationship and what you want in business, and they are probably not the same. Your values about what you want in one or in the other may be quite different. (Actually, if they're not, it's possible that you may have trouble with both.) Since values are context related they can also be state related, although values are definitely less related to state than are beliefs.

BELIEFS

The next level of filters are beliefs. Beliefs are convictions or acceptances that certain things are true or real. They are also generalizations about the state of the world. One of the more important elements in Modeling (which is an NLP process for recreating excellence; see Glossary) is to find a person's beliefs about the particular behavior we are trying to model. Richard Bandler says, "Beliefs are those things we can't get around." Beliefs are the presuppositions that we have about certain things that either create or deny personal power for us. At this level beliefs are essentially our on/off switches for our ability to do anything in the world, because if you don't believe you can do something, you probably won't have the opportunity to find out. In the process of working with someone's beliefs it is important to elicit or find out what beliefs he has that causes him to be able to do what he does. We also want to find out the disabling beliefs, the ones that do not allow them to do what they want to do.

ATTITUDES

Attitudes are collections of values and belief systems around a certain subject. We are usually quite conscious of our attitudes, and often tell people, "Well, that's just the way I feel about that." Change made on the level of attitude is often substantially harder than the level of values. (Have you ever tried to change someone's attitude?) It is far easier to change values than attitudes because of the level of abstraction.

MEMORIES

The fifth filter is our collection of memories. Memories deeply affect a person's perceptions and personality. They are who we are. In fact, some psychologists believe that as we get older our reactions in the present are reactions to gestalts (collections of memories that are organized in a certain way around a certain subject) of past memories and that the present plays very little part in our behavior.

DECISIONS

The sixth filter, which is also related to memories, are decisions that were made in the past. Decisions about who we are, especially limiting decisions, can affect our entire life. Decisions may create beliefs, values, attitudes and even life themes, or they may just affect our perceptions through time. The problem with many decisions is that they were made either unconsciously or at a very early age and forgotten. Also, we may decide at one point in time and then not re-evaluate our decisions as we grow and our values change. Those decisions that are not re-evaluated (especially the limiting ones) often affect our life in ways that we had not originally intended.

Decisions and memories vary throughout the range of conscious and unconscious. Individual decisions and memories may be found to be more or less conscious than certain values, beliefs and attitudes.

These six filters, then, determine what information is retained as we make an IR of any event. It is our IR that causes us to be in a certain "state" and creates a certain physiology. "State" refers to the internal emotional state of the individual—i.e., a happy state, a sad state, a motivated state, and so on. Our IR includes our internal pictures, sounds and dialogue, and our feelings (for example, whether we feel motivated, challenged, pleased, excited, and so on). The state in which we find ourselves determines our behavior. So the IR of the event combines with a physiology and creates a state. A given state is the result of the combination of an internal representation and a physiology. And all behavior is state-related.

So these filters, in a way, determine our actions, since what is retained or deleted will have a major effect on the IR. Why is it that two people can attend the same event, and one will love it, while the other hates it? The reason is because the IR is so dependent on the filters.

Remember that in this model the map (or the IR) is not the territory. Our every experience is something that we literally "make up" inside our heads. We experience reality indirectly, since we are always deleting, distorting and generalizing. Essentially, we experience our representation of the experience of the territory and not the territory itself.

In a study of communication at the University of Pennsylvania in 1970[*] the researchers determined that in communication, seven percent of what we communicate is the result of the words that we say, or of the content of our communication. Thirty-eight percent of our communication to others is a result of our verbal behavior, which includes tone of voice, timbre, tempo and volume. Fifty-five percent of our communication to others is a result of our non-verbal communication, i.e., our body posture, breathing, skin color and movement. The match between our verbal and non-verbal communication indicates the level of congruency.[†]

Our model for the Basis of Personality includes the following major elements that make up the personality:

THE TIME LINE

Who are we but our collection of memories? For years, psychologists have agreed that our past experiences do determine who we are and how we act. (Although the examination of memories has recently fallen into disfavor among psychologists because they did not know what to do with the memories or how to affect them.) Memories are recorded and stored as we age and with time, they have more and more influence. Our Time Line is the memory coding of the brain. It is how people encode and store their memories. Otherwise, how would you know the difference between a past memory and a future dream? With the discovery of Time Line, we also have, for the first time, the ability to change significant numbers of a person's memories in a short time. Obviously, changing a substantial number of a person's memories will have an impact on the person's personality.

---

[*]"Kinesics and Communication," R. Birdwhistle, University of Pennsylvania, 1970.

[†]See "Structure of Magic II" for a full description, Grinder, J., et al., Science and Behavior Books, 1976.)

In addition, our behavior is guided by decisions that we've made in the past. Whether conscious or unconscious, these decisions affect our behavior in the present. Our decisions are stored in the Time Line, and through Time Line we gain access to them.

META PROGRAMS

Meta Programs are the deepest level, content-free programs that filter our perception. Meta Programs serve the purpose of deletion and distortion, and they maintain or break our generalizations. There are four basic filters to perception that are our most basic Meta Programs. They are similar to Jung's personality types as outlined in the book *Psychological Types.*

The four simple filters then combine to produce roughly twenty or so complex filters. You may not have thought of it yet, but the question of whether "the glass is half empty or half full" is the result of one of these filters in operation. Meta Program filters do their work in a way that is independent of and devoid of any content. That is, they filter perception in a way that they do without regard to content.

VALUES AND BELIEFS

How people encode their most cherished values, beliefs and attitudes also has a profound effect on the personality. With background information on how values, beliefs and attitudes are formed, how they are encoded in the brain, and how people judge good and evil or right and wrong, we can also predict their internal states in reaction to certain situations, and therefore predict their behavior. Knowing this, we can also change their values. Values are primarily responsible for our motivation, and will determine how we spend our time. Values create the primary feelings that determine our motivation and therefore our actions. Values are how people choose and evaluate their actions.

Finally, inside the individual there are parts (minor personalities, or systems of values, if you will) that maintain the internal workings of the personality and tie all the elements together. We

---

Psychological Types, Jung, C., Princeton University Press, 1971.

believe that internal conflicts among the internal parts are responsible for many personality problems, including simple incongruities, as well as more severe health problems and personality disorders.

These are the elements that make up the personality in a normal, healthy human being (and even in those who are not). We include these elements in the Basis of Personality along with the means to make permanent and lasting changes in the individual.

The basic ideas in this book were originally developed by Dr. Richard Bandler, to whom we are indebted for his insight. Because much of this book was taken from transcripts of our teaching seminars, it may read more like the spoken word than the written word. We agonized over this question in the process of writing this book, and have decided that to rewrite the entire manuscript would delay this valuable information in reaching people who could really use it. And so with this caveat we offer you our model: Time Line, The Basis of Personality.

II

Time Line Therapy

1

Introduction to Time Line

Time Line is the first element in the Basis of Personality. It is a key element to an understanding of personality. Our memories, our decisions, our experiences good and bad are collected here over time and determine how we relate to the world. How we store memories affects how we experience our lives and how we experience time.

Now, time is something that fascinates me. I used to own a time management seminar company and that was a long time ago. I became really fascinated with the notions of goal setting and time management, and how time seems to work in some people's favor and against other people. I wondered about the nature of time. I read in the dictionary that time is an "... indefinite, unlimited duration in which things are considered as happening in the past, present and future." That didn't seem to help. It gave me a definition, but not the reason why.

I noticed that some people had all the time they needed while others did not. I noticed that some people seemed to be organized while others were not. I noticed that some people who set goals achieved their goals and others did not. I became more and more fascinated with the issue of time. I then learned about Meta Programs, which led me to the discovery that I had a Time Line! Lo and behold, so did other people! What an interesting idea! People DO have, inside them, a way of coding the past, present and the future so they know which is the past, which is the present and which is the future. You do, do you not? Otherwise how would you know that you already had paid your taxes, and didn't need to pay them again? Not knowing *that* might be horrible! Further, I am certain that the IRS would find a way to tax you again if you were unsure!! Fortunately you *do* know the difference between the past, present and future.

YOUR TIME LINE

If you were to stop and think about it, you might discover that you have your past arranged in a certain way so that you can tell the difference between it and the future. Otherwise, how would you know which event was in the past and which event was in the future? How would you know whether you were looking at a memory of the past or a memory of the future? But you *do* know the difference, you know. How you know is dependent on the way you encode the memories of past and future—it's how you store the information in your brain. Almost everyone stores time in a linear way, and *how* they store it makes the difference. Edward T. Hall says that this simple ability of knowing what is a real event (outside), and what is a remembered, or a made-up event, is necessary for our survival.

COMMUNICATION PATTERNS

Many of the language patterns that we use in NLP or that are used unconsciously by an excellent communicator are a result of knowing (either consciously or unconsciously) how people organize time inside their heads. I've also noticed that people who know how other people store time are much more facile in using temporal language shifts to produce changes and shifts in clients in therapy and business situations. You may have noticed that as people talk, they will often give you a description of what they are doing mentally. Could it be that this description is not metaphorical, but is literal? Have you ever heard someone say, "You're going to look back on this and laugh." Or how about, "Put it behind you," or "Time is on my side."

Well, we wondered, "What does this mean?" We now believe that the way people talk about their internal experience (including their gestures) of time is a literal (as opposed to a metaphorical) description of the composition of their experience. How people talk about time is an actual representation of what they do mentally. Use of temporal language is just a description of how they store time.

We will begin by describing the Time Line and how it works. First, a bit of theory. Then, how it works mentally and some exercises, and then an actual transcript of some demonstration change work. You will have the opportunity to see how it works in yourself and other people.

TIME STORAGE

Internal time storage is actually a fascinating subject. The notion of how time storage affects personality comes from a number of several different sources including Edward T. Hall's book, *The Dance of Life.** Hall talks about two kinds of time.

ANGLO-EUROPEAN TIME

Anglo-European time, as described by Hall, seems to have been born out of the Industrial Revolution. You see, back in the early days when factories were first built, people had to be on time. Why? Because if you started the assembly machines at 9:00 and half the people weren't there, then all the products would run off the end. (After all, who would put them in boxes?) Factory owners realized that they needed a system for getting people to the factory on time. The assembly line led to a notion of time as being linearly structured where one event happened after another. Thus, the Anglo-European notion of time has its roots in the Industrial Revolution and the assembly line, where there is one thing after another occurring in an orderly sequence or series of events that stretches from left to right (or vice versa) like an assembly line.

In the Anglo-European view of time, if, for example, we have an appointment at 9:00 and my next appointment is at 10:00, we meet for one hour alone. At 10:00 you and I are done whether or not we have completed everything. You and I are done and I go on to my 10:00 appointment. That is an example of the Anglo-European conception of time.

ARABIC TIME

Arabic, Islamic and other southern (warm climate) countries have a completely different notion of time—Islam, India and the

---

**The Dance of Life*, Edward T. Hall, 1984

southern regions like the South Pacific, Caribbean and even the southern United States have a completely different notion of time.

Their notion is that time is something that's happening now. If you and I have an appointment at 2:00, and you show up at 2:30, well that's OK, because I was doing other things anyway and I didn't really notice that you were late. If we start at 2:30, that's fine and we'll go on as long as it takes. If somebody else was expected to show up at 3:00, great!! When they do, they can sit in and watch us finish our first meeting.

The Caribbean and Mexico are famous for their notions of time, where if you say, "When are you going to have something done?" they say, "Well, tomorrow, manana." In Mexico, for example, if you say, "When are you going to have it done?" they'll say, "Well, you know, tomorrow, we'll get it done tomorrow." If you've dealt with this type of thinking about time, you know that "tomorrow" can be any time after the sun sets tonight and three weeks from now. And if you've ever spent time in Hawaii, you're probably familiar with Hawaiian Time, which is at least 30 minutes behind clock time.

When Westerners first go to countries like Iraq and have the first meeting with an Iraqui businessperson, they may be upset because the Iraqui businessperson might have nine or ten people meeting with him, and he will have discussions going simultaneously with all of them. The American businessperson will say, "But I was supposed to have a personal meeting." They'll say, "This IS a personal meeting."

MAJOR DIFFERENCES IN CONCEPT OF TIME

In the Arabic notion of time, since time is happening all at once and happening now, there is no real notion of a future. Arabic people are well known for not having a notion of time beyond two weeks from now. You see, future planning is not possible where all time is now and there's nothing beyond two weeks from now.

These are the two ways that people organize time. One is Anglo-European, where there are linear, sequential, planned events. The other is Arabic, where time is an all-at-once event. So people do have different notions of time. Now, in the Anglo-European notion of time, if you and I have an appointment, you expect to see me alone. In the Arabic view of time, if you and I have an appointment, don't expect to see me alone, expect to see me with three or four other people.

IN THE UNITED STATES

Now, in the United States both of these modes of experiencing time are operative. Edward Hall says that the American businessperson frequently runs on the Anglo-European model of time and the American housewife often runs on the Arabic model of time. She will typically handle all family members simultaneously, being in the now. The husband may say, "We're going out to the theater at 7:00," At 7:30 she may be putting on the last of her make up because she's finishing up, tucking the kids in and cleaning the kitchen. As soon as it's all done (doesn't matter how long it takes, when we're done, we're done) it's OK to go.

Interestingly enough, whether you use one or the other of these two models is totally determined by your internal coding system. We can discover how you store time by asking a simple question about how you code your memory storage of the events that make up your history and future internally.

HOW YOU STORE TIME

So what I would like you to do for a moment is to stop and think of where the past is and where the future is for you. When you stop to think of it, consider that memories in the past have a certain direction as they come to you. They are stored in a certain location so that you know the difference between them and the events that are in your future. Now, I also call events in your future memories. You'll see why in a moment. There are events out there in your future that are different from the events in your past, and you know this because you've got them organized differently. Now, if I were to ask you, "Could you point to the past and to the future?" if I were to say, "Can you point to the future?" to what direction would you point? To what direction do you point, when I ask, "Where's the past?" Did you point left to right, or front to back, up to down, or some other combination?

The Anglo-European type of time we call "Through Time," and it is delineated by a Time Line that stretches from left to right (or right to left), or any other organization where all the past, present, and future are in front of you. The Arabic type of time, which we call "In Time," is represented by a Time Line that stretches from front to back or any combination of past, present and future where a portion of the Time Line is inside your body, or behind the plane of your eyes.

DETERMINING TIME SORTS

When questioning someone to determine whether they are In Time or Through Time, you can ask several different questions. If you want to do it quickly, just say, "Where's the past and where's the future for you?" Or, "In what direction is your past, and in what direction is your future?" Roughly half the people you question will answer easily. Most people will have no problem discovering how they represent time, and will tell you, "My future is in front and the past is behind." Or they'll say that the future is left and the past is right, or they'll give you some other direction.

You may run across people who will give you a geographic location, saying, "San Bernadino." Don't laugh! It's true. "Where's your future?" "San Bernadino." OK! (I'll tell you that San Bernadino is a better place to be from than to be going to! Just kidding.) If that happens, work with them until they are able to formulate a linear pattern for their memories.

If they are unable to give you a direction when you say, "Where's the past and where's the future for you?" then say, "I'd like you to stop and recall a memory from when you were age..." and then pick an age. My favorite ages are somewhere around age 5 to 7, 10 to 13, and 16 to 18, and last week, depending on how old the person is. So you say, "What I'd like you to do is stop and recall a memory from the past." And then you say, "Now, what direction did that memory come to you from?" Then say, "Now, I'd like you to think of something that's going to happen in the future, say six months or a year from now... Now, from what direction did that memory come to you?" Notice in both cases I used the word "now." That keeps them oriented to the present. The word "now" is important there. It keeps them in the present, noticing the orientation of from where the memory came to them. Frequently you will have one of two possible responses.

THROUGH TIME

The Through Time (Anglo-European) person has his or her Time Line organized from left to right or from up to down or in a "v," or in some other organization where (and here's the critical component), the past, present and future are all in front of the person at all times without the person having to turn his or her head. The past and the future are in front of the person without the person having to turn his or her head to see it. For example, if the past is on the left, and in his or her peripheral vision, and the future is on the right, then the person is Through Time. A Through Time person has the past, present and the future, in front of him or her, and not inside his or her body.

IN TIME

An In Time person, on the other hand, has some of his or her memories of the past and the future behind him or her no matter how the Time Line is arranged. This person will have all or some of the characteristics ascribed to Arabic time. In making the distinction between In Time and Through Time, notice that whether the Time Line is up to down, front to back or in some other configuration, the most critical component here is determining if any part of the past, present or future memories are behind him or her so that he or she has to turn his or her head to see them, or is a part of the Time Line inside his or her body. If any part of the Time Line dissects the body, the person is In Time.

2

Through Time and In Time—The Two Types

As you begin to examine people's Time Lines, you will find that they will have their Time Lines organized in any number of ways. A person may be In Time, or Through Time, or a combination of both. I have even found that some people have their futures in front coming up to the present, close to the present and running across from left to right, to an unspecified amount of time in the past and the rest of it behind them—a combination of both. There are also spiral and loop arrangements and various combinations. Each arrangement will have an effect on the person and his perception of time. The arrangement of our memories and our future will have a predictable effect on our personality. To begin, the major distinction that you will want to make is, is part of the Time Line behind the person? If it is, then the person is In Time. If not, then he or she is Through Time.

THROUGH TIME

People who prefer to code time as Through Time will store their memories left to right, or right to left, or in any other way, so that all time is in front of them. Time is continuous and uninterrupted. It may be "long" for them. They are aware of duration. For a Through Time person, memories are usually dissociated. That is, they see themselves in the memory. The arrangement of the memories also amplifies the dissociation; since all their memories are always in front of them, they must be dissociated. Their memory is what we call temporally sequential—time for them is linear, it has a length that may seem long. Through Time people, for example, may perceive the value of a therapist or consultant as equivalent to the amount of time spent. They will want to get their money's worth in terms of your time. If you spend an hour and a half, they'll want two. For them time and value are often equivalent. "I paid my money and I deserve to get every minute that's coming to me. I want to get all the time I paid for..."

Through Time people are regularly on time, or know when they are late. If you have an appointment with a Through Time person at 2:00 and you show up at 2:05, you could be considered late! In Time people can also perceive lateness, and some even feel bad when late, but that is usually related to their placing a high value on timeliness. A Through Time person will have his time tracked out in linear events. Some Through Time people even know what time it is within a few minutes. My wife knows, and I'll tell you she knows what time it is 24 hours a day.

The saying, "Time is on my side" is a Through Time statement. There are some advantages to being Through Time. If all your time is constantly in front of you it serves as a reference. For example, the past is always there as a reference. That is great if the past experiences are positive ones. However, we worked with one Through Time person who had problems in the past, because the past was always there staring him in the face. This person had problems in the present because of his evaluative feelings about past problems.

A Through Time person stores his or her memories in a dissociated way. (That is, they see themselves in the memory, rather than looking through their own eyes.) They also may have difficulty in accessing a specific memory, since Through Time people often have collapsed several experiences into a single gestalt. (A gestalt is constructed memory that represents all memories of that type.) For example, if asked to recall a specific time when they were truly happy, they may have trouble because they have collapsed all happy times into a single experience.

From a business point of view, a bookkeeper who is Through Time will be better at staying on track and will probably have his work done on time. In bookkeeping, timeliness is important! He will have the tasks laid out for each day of the month, and he'll usually have it all done on time. A Through Time person is better at staying on track and better at staying with the task, on the job. However, someone who is Through Time can have less ability to focus in, and "be here now," than an In Time person. A Through Time person in a hectic environment may experience a problem concentrating. From a business point of view, this person may function poorly if he or she has to work in a chaotic environment.

The Through Time person looks upon work time as being different from play (work is meant to be serious) and will live a more orderly, decided, planned existence. The Through Time person says, "Plan your work and work your plan." They will usually establish deadlines in work, take the deadlines seriously and will expect others to do the same. They have a high need for closure—an urgency to "get the show on the road." There is a high degree of correlation between the Through Time person and Carl Jung's* description of a preference for the "judging" modes.

IN TIME

An In Time person will prefer to code his or her memories from front to back, up to down, in a "v" or any arrangement where part of the past, present or future is behind or inside him or her. This corresponds to the Arabic model that we talked about earlier. Usually In Time people will have part of their history, or future part of their Time Lines, unavailable to them, unless they turn their heads. It's where the saying, "You're going to look back on it and laugh," comes from. Or, "Put your past behind you." These are In Time sayings, a linguistic description of what goes on inside an In Time Person. Think of it; if the Through Time person had an event in the past with which he or she were not happy, he would not be able to "look back on it and laugh." Why? Because for Through Time people, memories are always right in front of them. On the other hand, the In Time person is likely to store the past behind and would be likely to use a phrase like, "Put your past behind you."

In accessing memories, In Time people go back to one memory or point in time and are in that memory, associated

---

*Carl Jung, *Psychological Types*, Princeton University Press, 1971.

(looking through their own eyes, and feeling the feelings). They can go right back to a certain point In Time. Then they are "just where they are." Since they are not as aware of duration, as a Through Time Person is, they can be caught up in the "now," and may have trouble ending a meeting or session. An In Time person often won't know that he is five minutes late. Some would not even know if a half hour had gone by. For example, if you had an appointment with an In Time person at 2:00 and you showed up at 2:15, you were probably not late by his standards. The dividing point between In Time and Through Time lateness is usually somewhere between 5 and 15 minutes. With an In Time person, if you show up 15 minutes late, you are reasonably on time. They may have even forgotten about the appointment, or may not have any idea that you are not there. They will not know.

An In Time person finds it a lot easier to "be here now." A Through Time person finds it hard to be here now because the past, present and future are always there, in front of them, whereas an In Time person is here, in the now. Right in the now. "Be here now" is an In Time idea, because most In Time people are in the now all the time. In Time people frequently find it very easy to focus in and stay totally focused even in a chaotic situation, unlike their Through Time counterparts.

In Time people can seem to be undependable. They need open-endedness, and prefer to keep their options open, so they often resist making a decision because they suspect that it will limit their options. When they do decide, say in a selling situation, they may then have buyer's remorse because they fear that they have somehow limited their options. They may need someone to keep them on track, since they can have poorer concentration over time, such as in a long-term project. They often have trouble sorting out tasks.

In Time people can, however, go to the past and stay there more easily, because their memories are associated. In Time people can usually go back to a specific time easily, so they can be anchored in a fully associated state more easily. If they have not kept an agreement they may say, "That wasn't me," or "I wasn't myself." In therapy they may have a different problem every week.

The In Time person often looks upon work time and play time as being the same—and work is usually play. The In Time person will live a less orderly, more spontaneous, flexible, open-ended existence. The In Time person doesn't plan, preferring to "take it as it comes," adapting to life as he or she goes through it. Usually, they avoid setting deadlines. If they are faced with a deadline, they may establish artificially early deadlines. (Driving their Through Time associates crazy!) They display a high need to maintain their options, and avoid closure. There is a high degree of correlation between the In Time person and Carl Jung's[*] preference for the modes of "perceiving."

GESTALT

Our memories as we store them are arranged in a gestalt, which means simply that memories around a certain subject are often connected like a string of pearls might be connected. (See Diagram #2.) The gestalting of memories often takes place around a certain subject. The impact of the gestalt is that accessing a gestalt will often bring up a constructed memory that is a synthesis of all memories on the certain subject. Because of this, it is often harder for the person to access a specific memory.

In understanding Time Line Therapy™ it is important to understand that *both* In and Through Time people arrange their memories in a gestalt. Through Time people will be more influenced by it because all their memories are in front of them, and the gestalt is therefore more obvious. Since Through Time people typically access a gestalt instead of a particular memory, when you say, "I'd like you to go back to a time. Can you go back to a specific time and remember a time when..." the Through Time person could say to you, "Gosh, I can think of times when I was happy or motivated. I can think of motivating times, but not a specific time." This is because the Through Time person has collapsed all his or her memories into a single gestalt of motivating events. In other words, they make a collection of memories in a chain called "motivation" or called "happiness," etc. The gestalt occurs with In Time people too. The reason it is more noticeable in Through Time people is because all the time is in front of them.

---

[*]Carl Jung, *Psychological Types*, Princeton University Press, 1971.

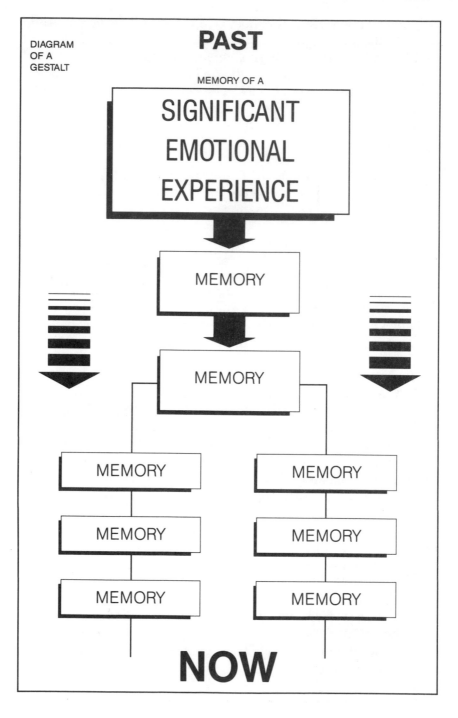

If the gestalt interferes with a Through Time person's accessing of a particular memory and he experiences trouble going back to a specific event, you can say to him or her, "What I would like you to do now is to turn the pages of your memory backward like a book. Turn the pages of your memory backward like a book until you come to that specific time when…" Likewise, if an In Time person has trouble getting back to a specific event, say, "What I would like you to do is rewind the movie of your life." You see, if the memories are arranged from left to right, then the analogy of a book works well. If the memories are arranged front to back then a movie analogy works better.

One of the more important notions about time, perhaps, is learning how to utilize the particular way people organize their time, so that you are able to establish rapport with the person and create change.

YOUR TIME LINE

What I'd like you to do again, is stop… and consider how you organize your time. You might consider your memories of the past and you might consider your memories of the future. I call them memories and you will see why in just a moment. If you think about it, you have a way of knowing that the past is the past and the future is the future. You see, your brain organizes memories in a certain way. So we are actually investigating the language of the brain, specifically how your brain organizes the past and the future, so you know which memory is in the past and which memory is an event in the future.

First, I'd like you to think of something that happened in the past and notice from what direction it came. And now I'd like you to think of something that's going to happen in the future or that you think will happen in the future and notice from what direction it came to you. Now, again, point to the future and the past, so you can have a sense of how you have your memories organized.

3

Discovering The Time Line

Transcript of Time Line elicitation:

Tad: "So, Dan, can you remember when you were five?"

Dan: "Yeah."

Tad: "Yeah. From what direction did that come to you?"

Dan: "Here."

Tad: "Good, is that behind you?"

Dan: "No, on the side of me." (Points to the left side.)

Tad: "On the side of you. When you look over in that direction, do you see all your memories from the past?"

Dan: (Surprised) "Oh, yeah."

Tad: "You see a bunch of memories over there on the left side?"

Dan: "Yeah."

Tad: "Good. So your past is on the left, and where's the future?"

Dan: "Over here on the right."

Tad: "And do you see future memories over there?"

Dan: "Yes."

Tad: "So, are you aware that the memories of the past and the memories of the future are arranged in a line that goes from left to the right?"

Dan: "Yes."

Tad: "That is your Time Line."

GROUP TIME LINE (TRANSCRIPT)

"OK, now, let's have some fun because that's what we're doing. What I'd like you to do is to stop, and to think about... You could actually stop and float up above your Time Line so that you have the opportunity to see the entire continuum of past, present and future below you as though it were organized in a line. And as you think about it, notice how good it feels to be above all that. You do, don't you? Excellent.

"Now, I'd like you to float back in time remembering, of course, where now is... and I'd like you to go back in time... and pick out a memory in the past that made you very happy... and drop right down into that memory and relive that experience. Step into your body, see what you saw, hear what you heard and feel the feelings of being in that happy memory. Isn't that good? But enough of this happiness. Putting that memory aside, now, for a moment, just put it right back in your Time Line where it was. Excellent!

"I'd like you to float up above your Time Line again. And I'd like you to look at the continuum of past, present and future. Get up high enough so you can see the whole thing now. This time I'd like you to float out all the way into the future. Just go right up to just before the end of the future of your Time Line and turn around and look back toward now. You're standing above your Time Line looking down on it so that you're looking back all the way from the future, all the way across now, all the way into the past.

"I want you to notice if the past and the present and the future have the same brightness. If they do, nod your head 'yes.' If the past, present and future do not have the same brightness, nod your head 'no.' If the future is darker than the past, nod your head 'yes.'

"Now, let's float back and take a memory from the past that's not really very important. Now, some people try to fool me when I say things like that. They say, 'Well I'll just take the biggest event,' and that is not what we want for this exercise. Take something that is really light-weight—a memory that you don't care about for now, for purposes of this experiment, and I'd like you to take that memory out of the Time Line, lock, stock and barrel. I mean the whole memory. Just take it right out of the Time Line, and stick it out in front of you and push it farther away than it is now, and farther, and farther, and farther. And make it darker as it goes, speeding away until it blows up into the sun. Now there's a gap in your Time Line where that memory was. And you can make up a new memory, now, that makes you feel very good about yourself, one where you're like the way you want to be. Now, I'd like you to put that new memory in the Time Line where the other memory was. Excellent.

"When you've done that, take all the time you need and then float up above your Time Line, now. As you do, notice how good it feels to be above all that, and float toward now. And this time I'd like you to go out into the future, to an event that you want to have happened. Find something that you would like to have happened in the future, something you really want. You might want to check and see if you lick your lips when you find this particular event. Richard Bandler always says, "If they don't lick their lips, it's not compelling enough." That's OK, we don't need a super-compelling experience yet. Just an experience that you want. We'll show you how to make it more compelling. Just take something you want, you like to have.

"By the way, notice that, just like the past events, there are future events in your Time Line, too. What does that say about your ability to have what you want? What if the future events are already there and all that happens is that 'now' just moves along your Time Line? How about that? What does that say about your ability to program the future so you can be having whatever you want? Now, wouldn't that be exciting?

"Can you pull up this outcome or event that you really want, and step into your body if you are not already there, and feel the feelings of having what you want? Now, take whatever it is that makes this memory of the future more compelling for you— turn up the brightness and make it brighter. Some people turn down the brightness and it becomes more compelling. Some people turn it up. I want you to do whatever you need to do to make it more real, so you really want it! Bring it closer. Bring it close enough so that it makes you feel really good. Yes, and make it more focused and clearer and sharper. Excellent. Just one more time, feel the feelings of being able to have whatever you want.

"Now, take that event and put it in the Time Line. As you put it in the Time Line, step out of the picture so you see your body in the picture and then put the event back in your Time Line, and notice that the work on the one event in the future has affected all the events between now and that event in the future. As you stand in the future, looking back toward now, notice that the events from then to now have changed to support the compellingness of that event. Notice how it happens automatically. Excellent.

"Now, what I'd like you to do when you're ready... Not yet, but when you're ready, is to float back toward now, float right down into now, and open your eyes. You can come back now whenever you're ready. Did you notice that making the event more compelling changed the gestalt of events going back toward now? Good. Now, you may or may not have noticed it, but what happens is that any changing of a future event will change the events in the gestalt." More about future programming in a later chapter.

4

Memory Management

Now you have some experience with your Time Line. You've had the experience of taking a future event and making it more compelling. You've also experienced taking an event from the past and throwing it away. That is memory management, by the way. Do you think you could take memories out of the past that made you unhappy? Yes. Could you do a complete change of your personal history using this model? Yes. Would it be quicker than using anchoring (see glossary) and going back to the event and changing the event? Yes. Does it cause major paradigm shifts and personality shifts in people if that's your choice? Yes, that's what it does.

It works, because we go back and change many events by changing one event. You noticed the gestalt changed when the event in the future was changed. If you go back and change the most significant event in the past, it also has the same effect.

THE PHOBIA MODEL

Let's see how this might be used in a phobia that a client presents to you. Suppose a client comes to you and says, "I've got a phobia." You say, "Great. Can you float up above your Time Line?" "Yes." "Go back into your past and recall the earliest time that you can remember this event." Now, you run the Phobia Model on the event. What is the Phobia Model?* Essentially the process is this:

1. Run the memory in black and white, dissociated (seeing your body in the picture), on the movie screen, run it out to the end.

2. Then freeze frame, and white it out (turning up the brightness), or black it out (turning the brightness down).

---

*For a full description of the Phobia Model, see *Magic in Action* by Richard Bandler.

3. Then run the movie in color backwards to the beginning, looking through your own eyes.

4. Do a swish pattern,* using how you used to act in the phobia situation as the old picture, and how you want to act in the future as the new picture.*

The phobia model is described more fully in the book *Using Your Brain For A Change*. It's also described in the book *Magic In Action*. There is a full description there, and under any circumstances, it is a must-read.

Using the Phobia Model with Time Line, when you change the major memory in a gestalt, you will change many more memories. The way I discovered this was by working with someone who had a mouse phobia, using the Time Line as the referential point. So what does it do? First, it dissociates the client completely. Second, it tends to change the whole gestalt more easily.

THE GESTALT

When you keep people up above their Time Lines and run the double dissociated Phobia Model where they're outside their bodies watching the event, it will change the entire gestalt. That is, it will change the events backward and forward from the event in the past by changing one event. If you change the major event, the other events that are connected to that event in the gestalt will automatically change. I'd like you to think of it as a chain, with one major event that connects a whole chain of events.

Some personal development programs talk about people being "reactive" when, for example, someone looks at them in a certain way and their responses are negative. What is happening is that they are flashing back to a gestalt of earlier memories that caused them to react negatively to that particular look. A chain of past memories has been accessed by that look in the present. Using Time Line, we can change people's past memories, or detach the emotion, and change their reactions in the future so they have control over their present. If I look at someone here in a certain way, and I go, "Mmm," and he freaks out, he or she has no

---

*See *Using Your Brain for a Change*, by Richard Bandler

control over his present emotions. If we change the past, we will get rid of his reaction.

Now, you can also *suggest* gestalt changes too. If you're doing a Phobia Model, or changing personal history, it's most effective to suggest that, "You might also notice that as you change this event, other events both forward and backward in your Time Line are changing or disappearing too!"

REPLACE DELETED MEMORIES

Another aspect of Time Line that is important is that when you take an event out of the past, you need to replace it. Earlier, we took an event that didn't matter out of your past, AND we replaced it. You must replace the event or the event may regenerate. In other words, if there is an empty pocket in your Time Line, the brain can regenerate the event.

DARK AREAS

At present, and maybe it is because the problem of child abuse is becoming more and more acceptable to talk about, more and more people are coming to me with major gaps in their past. Several people have said to me, "You know, I've got gaps in my past." If you float somebody above his Time Line and you say to him, "I'd like you to look at the continuum of past, present and future and notice if the brightness is the same," someone who's been abused in the past will have gaps in his Time Line or dark spots or dark areas. Dark areas, dark spots, or gaps are an indication of trauma, and it takes a lot of energy to keep the brightness down on the memories. Somebody who is keeping his past dark is going to use up a lot of energy. Bringing up the brightness on the past is going to release the energy used for that, and will usually give the person more energy to put toward what is wanted in the future.

If you ask them to brighten up their history or brighten up that particular event, they may not be able to do it easily. So what you say is, "Take an event that is unimportant to you. Make it darker, turn down the brightness. Can you do that?" "Yes." "Now, turn up the brightness. Can you do that?" "Yes." "Now, just like you did that, can you turn up the brightness on those events in the past that are dark?" If they still cannot, it might be that a part of them is keeping those events hidden. If that is the case you should proceed with caution because you may be uncovering major traumatic events from their past.

In the work on the mouse phobia mentioned earlier, all the memories had to be deleted. As long as the memories existed, there remained the possibility of her going back and getting reactive about mice. I would say, "Mice," and she'd freak out. So I took all the memories out. I took them out of her past and replaced them with other memories of her acting the way she wanted to around mice. In essence, we installed a new strategy during her Imprint Period. (See section on values.)

UNCONSCIOUS PERMISSION TO REMEMBER

Now, in the case, for example, of a traumatic event, I'll ask both the conscious and the unconscious mind the following: "Is it appropriate to remember the event?" You see, one of the things about traumas and phobias is that there are some learnings that have occurred where part of them is protecting or that part of them needs to remember.

PRESERVE LEARNINGS

Before you make major changes to the past, I would like to suggest that you will also want to say to the person something like, "Before we change this memory completely, you know that you learned something from that event, and it's important to learn from the past, so I'd like to ask you to preserve the learnings. You can preserve the things you learned from this event in the special place that you reserve for all such learnings." By the way, I don't know if there is a special place, but if it sounds right, they'll put it there. If they do not have one, they can make one. They will, I promise. Prior to making substantial changes to a memory, remember to preserve the learnings in that special place that they reserve for all those learnings. After you've done that, go ahead and take out the memory. In some trauma cases it is not appropriate or not necessary to take out the memory completely.

You have to check with the client in each case. If someone, for example, has been raped, you must preserve the learnings for her so that she can make sure that she knows the next time what the signs are. Then you may or you may not want to take out the memory. We don't want her to have to go through the same experiences to acquire the same knowledge, do we? No. Whereas, in some cases, like a mouse phobia, what's to learn? You can say, "Preserve the learnings, put them in that special place," and then destroy the memory. It depends on what's more appropriate and ecological. It is essential to check with the client's conscious and unconscious mind in an appropriate manner.

A NEW STRATEGY

Sometimes you will have to go so far as to install a new strategy for dealing with mice, for example. In that particular case, I had to give the client a new strategy for how to react to mice. She didn't have one. She had had a mouse phobia since age three. So you may need to build a new strategy. Her original strategy did not work. So a new one was in order. The original strategy was, "See something that looks like a mouse (Visual external), panic (Kinesthetic internal)." In fact, it was a two-step strategy where an external event (Visual external) caused an immediate response (Kinesthetic internal) in her. This two-step strategy is called a synesthesia. Usually the two steps are so closely linked that many times the person doesn't realize what's happening.

When we were finished, her new strategy was (1) see something that looks like a mouse (2) kinesthetic panic (3) see that it really is a mouse (4) kinesthetic relief (5) auditory—"Oh, it's only a mouse." (And when you think of all the things it could be...) "Oh, it's only a mouse." I installed that strategy and saw that it worked. Next, I went back and installed that strategy in her history. She only had to put it in there once because it created a whole new gestalt. It created a new chain, because the original gestalt was open since I had already destroyed it. Now she had a new operative strategy: "Oh, there's a mouse. That's only a mouse. Could have been something worse." The first week she went to a neighbor's house and held a pet mouse. Before the therapy she would not even go into her neighbor's house, or into any house where she thought there were mice. Of course, she did not remember the content of the therapy.

This is another thing that may happen in Time Line Therapy, and we see this in a number of our follow-up interviews where former clients are asked "What we do," and they'll say, "Gee, I don't know, but I feel better." Or, "It seems to work now and I'm totally different." That can happen when you're making major changes such as this. That's because being above the Time Line is literally Milton Erickson's "the middle of nowhere." (Milton Erickson, until his death in 1980, was the world's foremost hypnotherapist. He had the reputation for being able to hypnotize anybody, and he did.) Remember, Erickson used to tell his clients to meet him in the middle of nowhere. He would say, "I want you to become a bodiless mind floating in space." His clients did it! Amazing, especially because they had no comprehension of the location of "nowhere." So the Time Line is the same thing, when you think of it. Floating above your Time Line is the same as the middle of nowhere. But even more so.

THE CREATION OF BASIC MEMORIES AND PERSONALITY

How are basic memories created? (See the "Creation of Values" chapter for a further explanation). There are three periods. The first is the Imprint Period, where a child is like a sponge. The child soaks up and imprints all the events that occur: sights, sounds, feelings, tastes and smells. The Imprint Period is from approximately age birth to age 7. Then comes the Modeling Period, where a child models its parents and other people whom the child admires. That happens from age 8 to 13. Then there's the socialization period, where the teen says, "Hey, I'm a social being, I'm going to go outside the family and meet people." Now the complex social process called "dating" starts, and it begins during the Socialization Period, which occurs from 14 through age 21. Our social values are created at this time. These are the three major periods where the events in our lives create our values and our personality. Frequently, the groundwork for a phobia is laid during the Imprint Period. Phobias often have their origins before age 7, whether the client is aware of it or not.

When treating people using Time Line, you can truly make major changes in their personality by making changes in their history. Using this particular model, making individual changes in memories will change an entire gestalt. It changes a person's entire history in a matter of minutes—a very fast and effective procedure for making change.

5

Language and Time, The Meaning of Words

EMOTIONS

This leads to the next subject, emotions and the meaning of words as relates to time. One of the things I want you to consider is that many emotions have their meaning totally tied up in time. For example, guilt is an emotion of the past.

GUILT AND SHAME

Can you think of something you are guilty about? Choose, if you will, a mild form of guilt for purposes of this exercise. Now, let me just tell you in advance, what we're going to do is to non-verbally destroy the complex equivalence for guilt for this event. In other words, I'm not going to say anything to you about it. I'm just going to ask you a question. I'm not even going to tell you anything. You know enough about guilt already.

I'd like you to choose an event about which you were guilty. Got one? Pick something about which you were guilty, and if you can't find that, how about something that you are ashamed of? Shame is another emotion similar to guilt. All right, then, if you have nothing to be ashamed of, or guilty about, you should be guilty about that, by the way. Now, if you have discovered something near to lightweight guilt, I'd like you to float up above your Time Line. I'd like you to go back to one minute before the event about which you are guilty happened. Go back to one minute before the event about which you feel guilty and consider this question: **Now, where's the guilt?** How many of you found that you were laughing? Do you still have the guilt? Some will say, "It's right in front of me." If that is what they say, then say , "is it in front of you, or is it **gone now**?" That will destroy the guilt of an event for almost everyone. If the guilt is still remaining, then there is a part that needs to be reframed. Ask that part if it is all right for you to assist it to accomplish its intentions more easily, while allowing you to expand your capabilities? Good. Now, looking along your Time Line toward now, **now, where's the guilt**? All gone. Good. Come on back to now. Float down into now and open your eyes.

When doing Time Line, if the guilt does not disappear, then a part of the person needs to be reframed. A part thinks it is important to be guilty, and probably that part has provided certain positive intentions for the person. So you say, "I appreciate the part's desire to provide certain positive intentions for you all these years. And I wonder if you'd be willing to learn new ways of accomplishing your same intention, while discovering new ways to do it better and more easily in the future, learning how to create your life, being better and better, and if you can do that now, wouldn't you be willing to let go of the guilt while preserving the learnings?" And if that part says, "Yes," then we are off and running.

Guilt and shame are totally related to time. They have no existence outside of time. By the way, guilt and shame are two of the worst emotions on the planet. Let's get rid of them—they're worthless emotions. They're not at all valuable. I mean, people don't *need* to be guilty. Guilt and shame may occasionally play an important part in keeping a person from doing things they should not do. If that is the case, then new values and other guidelines for action may have to be installed before you destroy the guilt. (Of course, before you destroy anyone's guilt, make sure that you are not destroying guilt that serves the purpose of making the person perform right actions in the future. For example, destroying guilt for a criminal probably would not be the best thing, especially if the guilt was stopping him or her from committing the crime again.)

Imagine a client who comes to you and says (this really happened to me), "I'm compelled to please everybody all the time." "Why?" "Because I might feel guilty." "Good, can you remember an event you feel guilty about?" "Yes." "Good, float back to one minute before the event." This is very important. The language is very important in this. The next thing you say to them is, "Now, where's the guilt?" What does that do? It leaves them oriented in the now. "Now…" See, they're floating back, they're one minute before the event, but now, where's the guilt? They'll laugh. I guarantee you, they'll laugh. The first time you do this with somebody, they'll go, "Ha, ha, ha." If you do this three times on three different events, they'll probably laugh harder, and all their guilt will be gone. Good-bye guilt!

FEAR AND ANXIETY

Now, how about anxiety? Do you have anxiety? Or fear? People without guilt usually have fear or anxiety. Anxiety and fear are similar. Fear has an object (something to be afraid of) and anxiety is about an uncertain future. Anxiety, fear and guilt have no meaning outside of time. If you would, I'd like you to think of an event about which you're fearful—fearful or have anxiety about. When you have one, I'd like you to float up above your Time Line again. Go out into the future—one minute after the successful completion of the event about which you were anxious. (Of course, make sure that the event turns out the way you want.) And I'd like you to turn and look toward now. **Now, where's the anxiety?** Notice how you chuckle. Fear and anxiety have no existence outside of time.

Oh, no! Guess what? Time has no existence either. (I'm not going to tell you that, am I?) It's true. If fear and anxiety have no existence outside of time, what does that say about time? We won't say that yet, though. Just save that for a future thought. But I'd like you to consider it.

By the way, I usually try to make sure, not yet, but I usually try to make sure that people are out of the trance when I complete the session with them. And we're not complete yet, so…

TEMPORAL LANGUAGE

The *language* of time is also very powerful. Knowing how people store time internally allows you to match their internal world and then to change it.

This happened to me recently. A fellow came up to me and said, "I have this problem." I said, "Well, I really don't have my appointment calendar with me. Can you explain the problem to me?" He did, and I said, "Well, come to me tomorrow when I have my book with me and we'll make an appointment tomorrow." Then I did some time shifts—used temporal language to loosen up his hold on reality and embedded the language for change. He came back to me the next day and said, "You know, it's funny, but all those things seem to have cleared up without you. So I don't need to meet with you." And I said, "Oh, gosh, that's too bad."

Richard Bandler was the first person, to my knowledge, to make extensive use of temporal language. The following statement builds on his work. What I said to the above client probably sounded something like this (possible analog markings are in **boldface**):

"Go inside and **try in vain** to have the same problem. It **was** a terrible problem, **wasn't** it?

"You want to **make changes**, haven't you?... What would it be like when you have made those **changes, now**? In the future as you look back and see what it was like to have had that problem... as you **think about it now**, if you could **make this change** for yourself so that **you could STOP**... having **made that change** and see yourself **now**. Do you like the way you look if you could **make that change** and look back at yourself having made that **change now**!"

6

Your Client's Internal Representation of Time

I would like to suggest that you investigate your client's Time Line fully by making sure you know how the client stores time inside, because much of the time people will have different time storage than you do. So it's always important to check.

In order for Time Line Therapy™ to work best, you will want to make sure you're matching the client's internal experience. Time Line is exquisite because it is a trance induction, or at least it presupposes trance. When doing Time Line, you do not have to fool around with a formal induction. You do not have to say, "Excuse me, I'd like to put you in a trance now. Could you uncross your legs and put your hands on your thighs?" Time Line allows your client to access a trance that will make those changes easier and easier, doesn't it?

TROUBLE FINDING THE TIME LINE

One possible problem in doing Time Line therapy is with people having trouble accessing and knowing where their past, present and future are. If this happens, you will have to take a little more time with them and ask them to recall a memory from age five (or any early memory).

Tad: "What direction does that come to you from?"

Subject: "I don't know."

Tad: "Can you recall a memory from age six? (Pause) Good, from what direction does that come to you?"

Subject: "I don't know."

Tad: "Well, the next time, can you notice from which direction it came to you?"

If they keep saying "I don't know", you can say, "I know there's a part of you that arranges all the time inside you. I'd like you to talk to that part and ask it if it's willing to participate and allow us, (slower tempo) for the purposes of this exercise only, to discover how time is stored for the purpose of making it easier for you to achieve your intention. "You're willing to do that, aren't you?" The answer is usually, "Yes, I am." Usually, that'll get it. If not, go for more rapport and if necessary, you can do a formal trance induction and then investigate their time recall.

CHANGING TIME SORTING

I do a lot of work with a client who had a "negative" past. He had done some things that he was certainly not proud of, to say the least, ending up in jail and so forth. He felt bad about himself. The work I did was seemingly ineffective, so finally I just had him put his past behind him. While the past was behind him, he was in great shape. One day, his past flipped back to Through Time, and I asked, "Where's your past? Put it behind you again." And it stayed there.

So, you can change the direction of your client's Time Line. All you need to do is float him above his Time Line, and ask him to change the angle and then float back down. It will usually stay that way.

Sometimes people have an elastic Time Line. So if they say, "Every time I put it there, it sort of flips out on the side or flips back the other way," you'd say, "Good, I'd like you to put an elastic band on the other end of it so that it will hold it in place this time when you float down in your Time Line." If he is in a light trance, you can ask him to do anything and he will do it. You can also use the following metaphor: "Do you know the sound that Tupperware™ makes when it seals?" As they are saying, "Yes," you say, "Just like that lock(ed) right in there." Or you can say, "Do you know the sound a Mercedes door makes as it closes?" As they are saying, "Yes," you say, "Just like that lock(ed) right in there." It really does not matter what metaphor you use; if it is consistent with his internal experience it will work.

CONSISTENT WITH THE CLIENTS TIME LINE

Many of you arrange your Time Lines In Time; many are Through Time. Some of you have both operative simultaneously. What you want to do in working with clients is to make sure you are consistent with their models when you ask them to go back to the past or in the direction of their past. The reason that you want to know how they organize it is so that you can be consistent with their models when giving them instructions or when you are using temporal language.

INTERESTING POSSIBILITIES

There are many interesting possibilities. Over the past several years of investigating Time Line we have found some intriguing internal models. Once we found someone whose past was in front of him. Was he conservative? Yes, he was! Was he resistant to change? You bet!

I discovered somebody recently in Honolulu whose future was in front of her, but around the center. Her Imprint Period, ages 0 to 7, was stored above her head! From 0 to 7 was up above her. Everything else in the past was stored out in front in the center. The future was off on the sides. To my way of thinking, that's not a very efficient way to organize past, present and future. But when I discovered she knew which was the past, and which was the future, I left it that way. She asked me if I could show her how to program her future. So I had her go out in the future and pick a memory and make it brighter. (See Programming Your Future, page 79.)

7

Handling Trauma

SUBMODALITIES OF TIME LINES

It is most useful for a person to have a Time Line with contiguous or similar brightness, color, etc. The Time Line should have similar brightness, for example, running from the past through the future, with the future perhaps a little brighter than the past. The past should not be black or substantially darker than the future. The future should not be black or substantially darker than the past. When there is trauma, usually there are some gaps, holes and dark spaces in their Time Lines. In fact, dark areas are a tipoff that there has been trauma in the past.

To a woman with a snake phobia I said, "Can you float above your Time Line?" Yes. "Can you find the memory?" Yes. "Now put that up on the screen." She said, "I can't visualize. I haven't seen pictures in my head since I was age four." (We are about to do a phobia model and she can't visualize! Oops!) So I asked, "What is the relationship between the brightness of your past, present and future?" She said, "There are a lot of dark chunks in my past." I said, "Turn up the brightness on them." She said, "I don't want to. There are a lot of things there I don't want to see." So I said, "Can you take them out of your Time Line, just for the purposes of this experiment? Can you put them aside, where you know where they are but they don't need to bother you, where you can put them away, and they will be OK? You can get them later, if you want to; but you may not want to." She said, "I can't do that." So I said, "Take one memory that doesn't matter out of your Time Line and put it on the side." She said, "I can do that." "What did you take?" "I took snow." "Just like you took snow out, all the others can **blow out now**." She said, "Wow, you just totally disarranged my filing system. All the black memories are on the side over there, so disorganized." I said, "Good, you can leave them there." Her whole being lightened up at that moment. I then did overlap. The process of overlap is moving from one representational system (from most favored to least favored) to another in order to help someone develop more flexibility in a certain representational system. She couldn't visualize, so I said, "Walk along the beach, feel the cool, wet sand in your toes, listen to the sound of the birds overhead, and now look down at your feet and what do you see?" She said, "Oh no, I'm seeing sand. This is the first time I've ever seen pictures in my head since I can remember." Then we took her back and did the Phobia Model with the Time Line, and she ran it perfectly.

Another woman called me on the phone and said, "I can't make decisions." I said, "Float above your Time Line. What's the relationship between the past, present and future?" She said her future was black, and the present and past were of a normal color. I said, "Good, can you turn up the brightness on the future?" She said, "I can't." "Can you turn the brightness up on an event that's not important?" "No, I can't." I said, "Can you find an event in the future?" "Yes." "Is it bright or dim?" She said, "It's moderate." I said, "Good. Can you turn the brightness down?" She said, "Yes." "Can you turn it up, so it's normal?" She said, "Yes." "Now can you turn all the events up?" She said, "Yes, I can." Great! That was the extent of the therapy. Three days later she called me and said, "I'm making decisions like a champ. I can't believe it. I'm totally decisive. I know exactly what I want and I am able to make decisions clearly and easily." All in just three minutes on the phone, turning up the brightness on her future. If your future was black, you wouldn't make decisions well either. Who wants to make decisions with a black future?

The submodalities of the Time Line regarding past, present and future make a major difference in present experience. Black holes and black areas in the past indicate a trauma or some kind of abuse or something similar in the past. If it is ecological, you might want to lighten it up. It takes a lot of energy to keep the past black. When you lighten up the past, you're also going to increase the person's ability to direct that energy (that they were using to hide past events) toward the future, toward what they want. It takes energy to keep the brightness down on those events. By turning up the brightness on those events, you give them more energy.

CAVEATS REGARDING TRAUMA

Let's discuss some warnings when dealing with traumatic events or abuse cases, because we've done a lot of work with abuse cases and there are some things you should know. Here are some caveats. First is that you want to make sure, when you work with someone who was a victim of rape or sexual abuse, that you give the woman or man the option of proceeding or not before discovering what happened. You can say, "In order to go back and run the Phobia Model on these events, you may have to remember the events." They don't remember the events now, but they have major chunks of their memory that are gone and that bothers them. That is why they are in therapy. You say, "What do you think it is?" and they say, "I think I was abused." Now, at that point, in order for them to clean it all up, they will have to run the Phobia Model on it, and to do that they will have to remember those events. When this happens, there may be discomfort as other events that were suppressed also begin to surface and sort themselves out. So you want to say to the client, "If we do this therapy, then there may be periods of time where there may be some discomfort, or there may not. Is that all right?" (Let me tell you something, there will be. But all you say is that there may be or there may not be.) Give them a choice, so that they understand by making these changes, they may have to go through discomfort that may occur as the unconscious mind begins to sort out the memories. You want to get certainty, both conscious and unconscious agreement, before you proceed. The Time Line is certainly more benign than other kinds of therapy, including traditional hypnotherapy. Without the Time Line process, a person may have to go through a year or more of old memories coming up. Using Time Line we can complete it quickly.

Using Time Line for abuse therapy requires only a very short period of adjustment. The procedure is to take out the memory, taking out the gestalt if necessary, and then to replace it. If it is appropriate, you can take out the whole episode or at least change their personal history. Then the whole incident will be able to be normalized fairly quickly, or there may be a short period of adjustment. Some of the experiences may be oppressive, so you will want to make sure to give your client a choice. Now, with all that out of the way, go back and run a phobia cure model with the abused person, or you can go back and change his personal history, and you will have resolved the matter.

DETACHING EMOTIONS

One of the other things I often like to do beforehand is to detach the emotional content of the memories. I'll say something like this: "When you think of a specific event that is particularly unhappy for you, **it's OK** for you to continue to **remember that event**, but perhaps you'd like to have the emotions **detached** from that event. As you think of that particular event, notice down at the lower right-hand corner a little hook there. What I'd like you to do is to **unhook the emotions** that are there, just unhook them. Now, **step out of the picture** and make sure you see yourself in the picture. Notice how that changes the event." After you've done it with one event, you can do it with many. If they have a lot of negative events in their Time Line, you can then say, "What I'd like you to do now is to take all the events in the past that you're not particularly happy about, unhook all the emotions that are there." And it does happen. They unhook the emotions. Then the memories that remain are informational rather than negatively emotional.

We believe that the past should be informational rather than negatively emotional. We have learnings from the past. It is important that we learned from those events, and we probably stored those learnings in that special place we reserve for all such learnings. It is also important to remember that the past does not have to be negatively emotional. It should be informational, and it should contain positive emotions.

Another possibility for deleting negative emotions is to put the person on the other side of the event from now. Shifting the temporal perspective in that way also will delete the negative emotion. (See "Guilt and Anxiety", pages 43-45.)

8

The Language of Time

That leads us to language. Once you know a person's Time Line, i.e., once you know how someone organizes his memories on a Time Line, you then can use temporal language without Time Line. Right? You could say, "So as you go out into the future, for example, if you were to do that now, and look back upon now, if you go out into the future to that event that you liked, that you wanted, remember that event we made compelling earlier?

"What I'd like you to do is bring up that event we made compelling earlier. If you could just stop and bring up that event and go out one minute after that event and look back toward now. Do you like the way you look, having made those changes? What would it be like as you look back upon now, having made those changes now? That you wanted to make, haven't you. You like the way you look, don't you? Because that's the you that's most compelling to you, isn't it? And those are the things you want to have. Now, don't you? Good; what I'd like you to do is to put that memory back in the future, make sure it's just as compelling and just as lower-lip-licking as it was before, and float back to now."

So what did I do? I shifted time (verb tense as to past, present and future) in the language I used in a way that, in order for you to make sense of what I was saying, required you to accept the presuppositions inherent in the sentences. The language presupposed change. The temporal shifts were also based on your experience on the Time Line.

Having in mind his Time Line, you can say, "Go out in the future and look back toward now." What does that mean? They are going to do it, however. Under the right conditions, they can't help but do it. Temporal shifts like that will also put them in a light trance, which assists the process of change. In addition, there are certain other verb tense shifts that you can make. For example, is there a difference between, "What is your problem?" and "What was your problem?" Recognizing the difference, notice that the first sentence assumes present and the second assumes the past. Obviously, you wouldn't want to say, "What will your problem be?" unless there was a specific purpose.

By shifting the verb tense in the sentences you are using, you can also make subtle shifts in your client's internal representations. Now, verb tense shifts alone are usually not enough to cause the entire change, but are usually sufficient to allow you to gain closure at the end of a therapy, and future pace the client. Also notice that the "-ing" suffix changes the internal representation. There is a big difference between, "What was the problem you had?" and "What was the problem you were having?" The former probably will cause a representation that is limited in time, such as a slide. The latter will probably cause a representation that is ongoing in time, such as a movie. So, as you are using temporal language with your client, you can form your sentences so that they presuppose the problem being already completed, cured. (Also see "Programming Your Future on Time Line", page 79.)

TIME LINE DEMONSTRATION

Good. Let's do a quick demo. Who wants to be a subject? Let's do some trauma. John? Thank you.

Tad: "You said that you had some events in the past that were dark. So, let's pick one that's moderate. I mean, let's pick one that's moderately traumatic, let's not pick a major one, let's pick an easy one to begin to work with. I want to make sure that as we talk about it that you are... that working on some of these events may cause other events that were hidden and buried to begin to come up and surface, and you may have to handle those. I'm wondering if you're willing to do that.

John: "Yes."

Tad: "Great. OK. And what I'd like you to do then is to float up above your Time Line. Where's your future? Right there, OK, good. Where's your past? (Moves out of John's Time Line.) OK. I don't want to get in the way. (Pause) I'd like you to float up above your Time Line and go back into the past and pick an event that is, you know, not a barn burner, something agreeable that we want to change, and it's dark. (John nods, "Yes.") OK, good.

"So as you stand outside of that event, looking down on it, you get a sense that that's an OK event to change? OK to bring up and sort of smooth out whatever things are there? (John nods, "Yes.") OK, good. So, you're floating up above your Time Line as you look down on it. Remember, you're above your Time Line, you're right here now. As you're floating up above your Time Line, I want you to make sure you stay right there, and since you have all the training that you know you have, you can do that, right? I'd like you to very slowly turn up the brightness on the event. Staying right here.

"OK. Now, staying above the Time Line, I'd like you to take the event and put it on the screen in front of you. Staying above your Time Line, I'd like you to create a screen in front of you, and bring that event right up on to the screen. And I want you to have it in black and white, the event. We're going to run the movie of the event out from the beginning at high speed, dissociated, so you see yourself up on the screen to the point of maximum emotion, just one moment past that point of maximum emotion. And when we get out to that point, I want you to freeze-frame and white it out.

"Now, turn the brightness back down, and I want you to associate it and run it backwards in color, associate, step into the picture, run it backwards in color at high speed right back to the beginning. Bang. OK. "Now, as you think about that event, is that event OK?"

John: "Much better. I was just sad, and I don't know why."

Tad: "You were just sad. And now are the emotions a lot less? So you feel a lot better about that event?"

John: "Yes, not totally."

Tad: "Not totally? OK. Would you like to run that again?"

John: "Yeah."

Tad: "OK, go ahead. (Pause) And now, because those things you learned... because those learnings are important to you... and you learned things from that experience... and you want to preserve those things that you learned... while yet allowing yourself in the future... now... to be able to have those things you want and not have to keep those. You can let them go now. Can't you?"

John: "Yes."

Tad: "Good. So, as you think about that event now, is it OK?"

John: "Yes."

Tad: "Completely OK?"

John: "Yes."

Tad: "Great. So put that event back in your Time Line. "

John: "Something just happened. I'm seeing that a difficulty, going back in the past in the Time Line, almost stops it. It gets very muddled and a lot of the Time Line is dark and strangled out like it's been S-curved around, and so it's hard... I see chunks of bright, but I know that on either side there's chunks of dark, you know, where it's curved around... and it just straightened out, so, it's cleared itself up."

Tad: "OK. Now, are there other events in your past that are as easy to handle as this one that you'd like to have cleared up at this point? And I know you're very quick at this, because you're probably one of the faster people I've ever seen doing this type of thing, and I'm wondering if you could do those all at once. Just sort of turn up the brightness and have them be OK simultaneously."

"Could you, for example, run all of the ones that needed to be dissociated so that they were OK simultaneously, maybe, one, two, three, four, five, however many there needed to be simultaneously, so that they were all OK? Now. You can do that, can't you? So now as you look at your Time Line, is it the same brightness all the way? Are there still some events in the past that are... (Pause)

John: "None real dark."

Tad: "None real dark? So they've lightened up considerably?"

John: "Yes."

Tad: "Good. Good for you. So you're doing the hook thing, detaching emotions, too?"

John: "Yes."

Tad: "Good. All right. OK. Good. And, notice how they begin to go by themselves without you having to do anything. Yeah. Notice how quickly they can all sort of line up. Notice how much easier it is to breathe. You seem to be becoming lighter, yeah, if your whole past lightens up."

John: "It's a real big difference. The future is getting real bright too."

Tad: "All right!"

John: "Wow."

Tad: "You can leave it that way if you want to. (Pause) So now, as you look at the entire continuum of past, present and future, is it OK?"

John: "Yeah, it's really good!"

Tad: "Good. Excellent. Now, one of the things you may begin to notice in future weeks is that all the energy that you were using to hold that past the way it was has now been lightened up and can begin to be applied to future things that you want. And you can use that to make things that you want more compelling and even more irresistible to the point where, even without your seeming to have to do anything, you can begin to produce results that are seemingly miraculous in the future, now, as you think about it."

John: "Yeah, that's really exciting."

Tad: "Very good. Good. OK, can you float back into the now? Before you put your Time Line away totally, at the moment, I'd like you to notice that there is a number of events all the way from the past into the future that have changed, the gestalt theory, if you will, and notice that those things that you've, in the past, now lightened up, that it's actually changed the future so that those things that you wanted are really becoming easier to get."

John: "Yes."

Tad: "Good. So, what will you have to do in the future now that you've done these things that you've wanted to?"

John: "I won't *do* much, but I don't have to, it's going to work anyhow. I'm going to put some more compelling stuff in there."

Tad: "Almost effortlessly?"

John: "Yeah."

Tad: "Excellent. OK, good. Come back to now and when you're ready, you can open your eyes."

Tad: "That's great. Give him a hand. (Pause) Now, those of you who were watching him, notice how, when we got all the dark stuff cleared up, how his entire being lightened up, took a deep breath, the breathing became easier. As I look at you, now, you're a lot lighter."

John: "It's a real difference."

Tad: "Excellent. Good. Good for you. Questions? Dan."

Dan: "When you said, 'He's the fastest person,' you were using language patterns and creating the fast person, weren't you?"

Tad: "Haven't we? And that's what Time Line is all about. You may discover this, here. Dan, you may discover that you're learning things already unconsciously that you had no idea that were coming so easily. In fact, in our trainings we are training the unconscious, haven't we?"

John: "My experience is. I felt the shift consciously, when I didn't do it consciously, it happened, it just happened. And I was very much aware, I mean, I saw the Time Line change and I became aware of a lightening effect, feeling better, feeling resolved, and almost simultaneously I'm not wanting to spend more time back there, I want to look to the future..."

Tad: "Because you didn't need to hold the brightness down any more, you could just let go. And when the brightness comes up, then where's the compellingness?"

John: "Right."

Tad: "It's in the future."

John: "And then I was also very willing to accept, which I generally (Pause) but I was very willing to accept... It was exactly right on, it matched my experience totally."

Tad: "Did you get that? And that's just matching his experience. That is your experience. And if you know someone's Time Line, and you've made the changes, it's going to be totally OK, and that's what temporal language patterns are about. That's excellent. I'm glad you pointed it out. Because it makes sense to the conscious and unconscious mind. The unconscious mind says far out, we made all these changes, let's go and make the rest of them, bang. We're done."

John: "... there was a lot of them running rapidly, so I felt like I was running fast... And I also recognized that it was speeded up, you sped it up further, I recognized that when it happened. Again, all this seemed totally natural so I had no need to prevent it or stop it. It was totally along the lines with what we were going for."

Tad: "Good work. All right, so that's a little demo on the Time Line therapy. It is my experience that Time Line is the most powerful therapy you can do. You can make major shifts in a very short period of time."

What do we do in NLP? We change personal history, which is totally applicable to Time Line. We do reframing. We do visual squash, or spatial reframe (see "Changing the Basis of Personality"). All fit very easily into the Time Line format. Use it and you'll get major personality shifts in people. Those things that were easy to learn are becoming easier and easier.

GENERALIZATION

One of the major questions in NLP is, "Does it generalize?" If I make a change in a person, does it generalize? Time Line changes tend to generalize better than any other model I have seen, because we are working on the history of the person. You see, we are nothing more or less than our collection of memories. If we change the memories, using Time Line, then we can change the person.

9

Time Line Therapy—
A Demonstration

Occasionally, when a client comes to me and we do Time Line Therapy, if we're working on "stuff" (a clinical term) that's very deep, often the client may think that the source is not in this lifetime. If the client thinks (consciously or unconsciously) that the source is not in this lifetime, then the results will not be as good, if I do not include the possibility of past lives. I realized the necessity of including past lives when modeling Dr. Chuck Spezzano, a Honolulu psychologist to whom I am indebted for the wording that follows.

To allow for the possibility of past lives, you might say, "Now, I could guess when the event was that caused this problem, but your unconscious mind knows better than you or I do. There was an event that was the cause of this... (condition or behavior) ... and if you were to know when you decided to have this... (condition or behavior) ... would it be before, during, or after your birth?"

If the client says that the event was before birth, then you can say, "Was it while you were in the womb or before?" (If you've already done some Time Line Therapy, you probably have found that many people can remember back to the womb. They remember events that happened and experiences that occurred while they were in the womb.) If the client says, "In the womb," then handle it as you would any other memory.

If the client says, "before birth," then there are two options: You can say, "Did it happen in a past life or was it passed down through your bloodline, genealogically?" If they say, "Past life," you can say, "If you were to know, how many lifetimes ago was it?" If they say, "genealogically," say, "If you were to know, how many generations ago was it?" (Before you float them back to past lives or past generations, if it's the first time, have them mark "now" with a big flag and tie a string around their toe so they can find their way back.)

Notice that using this kind of language does not imply the existence of past life experiences, but it does allow for it. If the client's answer indicates a belief in past lives or genealogy then you can utilize it and enter the client's model of the world. In many cases, regardless of whether or not you believe in past lives, you should allow for them in your client's beliefs, or you may not get the result you're looking for.

Using this model, it is possible to go back and clear up a number of events in the past (even "past lives" or ancestral) that are interfering with present time experiences and events.

Next is an example of how to use this in Time Line so that you can make Time Line Therapy produce to its fullest extent. The following is a demonstration of a Time Line therapeutic process based on the question of leadership. I asked a question in a Master Practitioner training about accepting your true role as a leader. If you're reading this and wondering if the content applies to you, it does. So, as I do the work, you could be the subject too, couldn't you? We are all one, anyway, aren't we?

Randy: (Client comes to the stage.) "I'm nervous."

Tad: "Good. Change is often accompanied by an experience of anticipation. (Laughter from both.) That is similar in a lot of ways to, but isn't exactly the same as, nervousness. But it's actually fun to anticipate growing, although not always comfortable, isn't it? (To the group) So, all right, you may want to get to where you can clearly see physiology shifts. I'll point them out. (To client) I hope it's OK for me to be teaching while I'm doing this."

Randy: "It's OK."

Tad: (To group) "I'm going to treat this as though it were therapy, and you should know that Randy and I had some discussions in the back of the room in the last half hour as I was deciding if he is the one who (to Randy) **you want to change, now**. (To group) So if I skip some of the basic up-front processes, like the standard NLP Well Formedness Conditions, and Achievable Outcome definitions, it's because I already have them. I especially want you to remember, when you are doing a Time Line Therapy, to make sure that you do all the standard NLP processes. If I skip something here, it's because I've already got it. (To Randy) If you were to say that there's something that you want to be complete with before you leave the chair, what would that be?

Randy: "Letting go of fearfulness for me to be successful."

Tad: "Good. OK. That's important to you?"

Randy: "Yes."

Tad: "OK. What is it that prevents you from being successful, right now?"

Randy: "Association to the past."

Tad: "OK. Was there a time when you decided that it wasn't OK to be successful? Do you remember that time?"

Randy: "OK."

Tad: "Can you float up above your Time Line and go back to that time, now? (Pause) Now, what I'd like you to do just for a moment is I'd like you to float right down into your body at the time and tell me what emotions were present at that time."

Randy: "Betrayal."

Tad: "OK. Float up above your Time Line again..."

Randy: "Can't I wallow in it for a minute?"

Tad: "Hey. You can wallow in it for as long as you want, but how long have you been there?"

Randy: "Too..."

Tad: "Too long."

Randy: "Yes."

Tad: "I mean so..."

Randy: "Enough."

Tad: "I mean, you can hold on to it as long as you want, and soon we're going to let it go. Yeah. OK. So, go back five minutes before that moment, float down just above your Time Line, turn back around, and look toward now as you look along the continuum toward now, and I want to ask you a question. (Pause) Now, where's the emotion of betrayal? (Pause) Gone?"

Randy: (Shakes head, no.)

Tad: "Now, I know that there may be a part of you that thinks it's necessary to hold on to that, so before you let *all* of it go, I want you to take all the things you learned from that betrayal, all the learnings that you have, and I'd like you to store them in that special place, that special place you reserve for all such learnings, the place that's important to you, where you can preserve those. 'Cause the things you learned were important, and it's OK to let that emotion go now... (Pause) haven't you? (Pause) ... still thinks it's important to hang on to that, and I'd like to ask that part to preserve those learnings, and make sure that it's willing to let that go. (Pause) So what does that do to the decision?"

Randy: "Um. Hum."

Tad: "Could we say that it has disappeared, and that you now... (Randy laughs) Could we say that it has disappeared and that you now have the choice to be successful? Now, I know you haven't chosen that (Pause) yet. But you've wanted to. I know you haven't chosen that just yet and we're not complete yet either, are we?"

Randy: "No."

Tad: "Not yet. So I want you to float back up above your Time Line, and often what happens when we do things like this is we work through different layers, uh, of things. So, I'd like you to, uh, look and see, at the moment, what else there is that would prevent you from being successful, if there were something in your past."

Randy: (Sarcastically) "That wasn't too much of a one, there though. Do you want one more?"

Tad: "Yes."

Randy: "Fear of being hated by my parents."

Tad: "Ah. I thought that there was something about parents there. OK. (Pause) So I'd like to talk to the part of you that's your father inside you, and I'd like to ask that part of you if he could possibly hate... (Pause) What does he say? (Pause) In fact, the fear..."

Randy: "He says, 'No of course not, you're my son.'"

Tad: "And how old were you when you decided that you were afraid of your father hating you?"

Randy: "About three... (Pause) no, two."

Tad: "Do you realize now that the fear of your father hating you was actually a mistake?"

Randy: "No."

Tad: (Surprised) "You don't realize that?"

Randy: "Um."

Tad: "Well, you don't need to yet. (Laughter) Uh, and I think it's important to have certain values around maintaining a relationship with your parents, and that perhaps this mistaken notion of your father hating you, because he says that he couldn't possibly... uh, so could you float up above your Time Line, now, and go back to age two, and float right down into your body at the time you decided that you could do anything that would cause your father to hate you, and what emotions are present there at the time?"

Randy: "I don't know if 'I don't want the son of a bitch to spank me,' is an emotion or not, but..."

Tad: "It's pretty close." (Pause) "Did he ever spank you?"

Randy: "Yes."

Tad: "Ask him, the part of you that is your father inside you, if he spanked you out of..."

Randy: "He was angry with his father."

Tad: "Uh huh. Great. I'd like you to ask the part of you that is your father, to ask the part of him that is his father if he could do anything other than love your father."

Randy: (Long pause) "He never wanted him."

Tad: "So, I'd like to ask the part of you that is your father's father to go back on his time line, to the time when he made that decision, and what emotions are present there when he made that decision?"

Randy: "That's a familiar one. Betrayal."

Tad: "Um. Does that say anything about..."

Randy: "Generation skipping?"

Tad: "A theme in a family? (Pause) I'd like to ask you now, how far back does this theme of betrayal go? In your bloodline. Pick whatever comes up. You know how to do this."

Randy: "A long way."

Tad: "Good. I'd like you to go back to that time in your family's time line, and if you were to know how many generations back the question of betrayal became an issue it would be..." (Pause)

Randy: "Forty."

Tad: "Good. I'd like you to go back to that time, to the ancestor of yours forty generations ago, where this betrayal started, and I'd like you to float, and I'd like you to have this ancestor of yours, male or female?"

Randy: "Female."

Tad: "Uh huh. Can you see her?"

Randy: (Nods yes.)

Tad: "Good job. I'd like you to have her notice what emotions are present when she decided that she had been betrayed." (Pause)

Randy: "Uh huh."

Tad: "Now I'd like you to have her go five minutes before, turn around and look toward now, along the 40 generations, across all those Time Lines..." (Pause)

Randy: (Smiles)

Tad: "That's right. Good job. Now, anything that she needs at this point? What would it be that she needs, if she needs something, and I know that she's already experienced that the emotion of betrayal has disappeared, is there something that she needs to be whole, and healed?"

Randy: "Love and comfort."

Tad: "Can you give that to her?"

Randy: "Uh huh."

Tad: "Can you allow that to come to you from a source outside yourself, from a source that is the source of all love and comfort, and flow from above the top of your head through you, across those forty generations, to her?"

Randy: "Yes."

Tad: "And what is the expression on her face now?"

Randy: "Do you want a mirror or do you want a description?"

Tad: "I got it already."

Randy: "I know you do."

Tad: (Laughter) "Now, I'd like you to look at her across those forty generations, and I'd like her to look at you across those forty generations, and notice that the issue of betrayal as a family issue has disappeared, (Pause) although there may still be events there. Now, is there any other healing that you need to do along that line of forty generations that will cause the question of betrayal to have been completely healed, now?" (Pause)

Randy: "No."

Tad: "Good job. Now what I'd like to have you do is to float back above your Time Line, and I appreciate those parts being willing to participate, and I appreciate their willingness to continue to grow and evolve in this direction, won't they, and discover new ways that they can continue to make those changes..." (Pause)

Randy: "She says, thank you."

Tad: "Yes. Tell her I appreciate her willingness to communicate with us and to be whole. And I'd like to talk to the part of you that is your father inside of you, around this issue of success, and I'd like to ask him if he's willing to give you his total unqualified support in your being a success, now, in the way that you want to be, because he loves you, and because that's what all fathers want for their children."

Randy: "You hooked him on that last one. (Pause) The last comment did it. 'That's because ALL,' and of course he followed right along."

Tad: "Yes. And does he notice that your grandfather wanted, as we've changed the, (whispers) that's right, Time Line, that he's now a wanted child and that changes everything, because ALL fathers want only the best for their children? (Pause) Does he notice that?"

Randy: "Notices it, yes. Doesn't totally believe it. Notices it."

Tad: "I'd like your grandfather, now that he's experienced a change in the history of the family, to have a conversation with your father, in a way that your father could feel (Pause) loved. (Pause) That's right. Good job. Could you have your grandfather put his arms around your father, inside you, and could you have at the same time, could you supply them with what they need to be whole inside you, and let it flow through you from the infinite source above you, so that they are healed in the best way possible, now? In a way that will be most productive for them, and easy to accept. What are they saying? Are they surprised?"

Randy: "Um huh."

Tad: "And are they congruent inside themselves that this is OK, now?"

Randy: (Nods)

Tad: "Good. Now, I'd like to talk to your father again if I may, and I appreciate his willingness to communicate, and I'd like to ask again if there's anything that prevents him from giving you the total unqualified support that fathers always give their sons even though they don't know it consciously all the time, but when they look inside, it's really always there, because a father wants so much for his son. I know you do. Father wants so much for his son, and sometimes it's hard to show, 'cause he's being a man (sniffs) and that's OK. Is it OK with him to be loved? Is there anything he needs, is there anything that your grandfather needs to be able to give you that unqualified support so that you can be a success, now? If there was something that they would still need what would that be?" (Pause) It would be..."

Randy: "It would be the knowledge that I would love them, (Laughs) after I became successful..."

Tad: "Now. (Pause) It's a fear isn't it? That that could be."

Randy: "Uh huh."

Tad: "And yet, could any son (Pause) not love his father? Not love his father. I mean deep inside, although on the surface (Laughter), because you see, what I want you to do is to look back and notice that all the events in the past, he was just doing the best he could do with what he had." (Pause)

Randy: "Yeah."

Tad: "Does he get that from you, as you communicate that to him?"

Randy: "As long as I say it a little bit different than I did just a few minutes ago."

Tad: "That's right. How would you say it to him so he'd really get it? Could you say it a little lower down with your voice? Could you say it with a little deeper tonality?"

Randy: "Yes."

Tad: "So that it was projected from here, (points to the area of Randy's heart) to him."

Randy: "I don't even want to not do that any more. Does that make sense?"

Tad: "Yes. (Pause) So, when are you going to be willing to let that go, now?"

Randy: "I already did."

Tad: "Good. That's beautiful. You're very good at this. (Laughter) Of course you have had some practice, and will continue, won't you, to grow in this direction, (Pause) now, what I want to know, as you look inside at your father, your grandfather, your part of you that was 40 generations back, do you notice the alignment that exists, that has occurred in there, in the generations that have come across, as you look at those Time Lines, a new alignment that perhaps you had not noticed before? Alignment's an interesting thing. It's like, you know the difference between those light bulbs (pointing to one of the standard lights in the room), and these (pointing to one of the TV lights)? And that's why a laser is so much brighter than a light bulb. Because all the light waves in a laser are totally aligned. A light bulb has light waves going in all directions, but a laser has light waves that are totally aligned. That's because it's got light that's totally… all the beams are totally lined up. Have you noticed that as you look along your Time Line, those forty generations? That there's a new alignment of purpose toward success, and those other things that you consider important to you. So now when you think of the issue of success, is there anything that prevents you from being successful? You see, you could let that go too."

Randy: "It was just a track. Just checking."

Tad: (Pause) "That's the one, what's that?"

Randy: (Laughs) "I'm just laughing because I know what you're doing to me at the time that you're doing it." (Laughter)

Tad: "That's the interesting thing about doing these things, and when you have them… you know, I had someone do a Time Line Therapy on me just the other day, it was really nice because I'd never had it done, and they said, 'Go back five minutes before,' and it disappeared. All those things I'd been holding on to just disappeared, like that, simultaneously, you know what I mean, don't you? (Laughter) So, as you think of it, now, and as you look out into your future, I want you to notice that some of those things, that some things that you wanted, you know, in the future are actually there in your Time Line (Pause) things that even a few minutes ago that you had to make an effort at getting, are now there in your Time Line, because you wanted them to be all along, and now they can be, can't they, aren't they? OK. Now, if there were one more thing, if there were one more thing that you had to let go of in order to assume the leadership role that you're going to assume one day anyway, now, (Pause) if there were just one more thing that you had to let go of, what would that be?"

Randy: "Fear of being shot."

Tad: "There was a time in your past..."

Randy: "I said fear of being shot."

Tad: "Yes. There was a time in your past when that this may have been an issue for you, if this happened to you once before in your past, would it be before, during, or after your birth?"

Randy: (Whispers) "Not this time."

Tad: "Was it in a previous lifetime that you were shot?"

Randy: "Yes."

Tad: "If you knew, it would be..."

Randy: "How much time do we have?"

Tad: "How much time do we need? We have all the time we need."

Randy: "Major ones. Three and four times ago."

Tad: "So, I want you to go back. I want you to float up above your Time Line this time, and I want you to float so far up above your Time Line and tie a string on this Time Line and attach it to your big toe. Put a nice bright flag at the end of your Time Line, one that you like the color of. I'd like you to float so far up above your time line that you begin to see the other Time Lines, and I'd like you to go back to the time three times or four times ago, or even the time when you created the issue that caused you to be shot at that time, I'd like you to go back to the root cause of that particular issue in time. Got it? (Pause) If you knew when it was, how many lifetimes ago would it be? It would be?"

Randy: "The root cause, I wasn't shot, I was stabbed."

Tad: "And how many lifetimes ago was that?"

Randy: "I'm just tracking to make sure. (Pause) Eighteen."

Tad: "Were you male or female?"

Randy: "Male."

Tad: "You've learned something clearly in this lifetime, and you have lots of learnings along the way. I'd like you to preserve all those learnings. You've learned some things that are extremely valuable, haven't you?"

Randy: (Crying) "Yes."

Tad: "And one of the things you've learned is how to have your sensory acuity high enough, 'cause we've talked about this. So, I'd like you to make an agreement with the part of you that's in charge of maintaining this sensory acuity at a high level at all times when it's appropriate for your protection, and I'd like to ask that part if it would be willing for us to just allow that part to do its work and achieve its intention more easily while we improve your past so that it can support you having those things that you want in the future. Now, it would be willing to do that, wouldn't it?"

Randy: "Yes."

Tad: "Good. So what I'd like you to do is I'd like you to go back now eighteen times ago to the moment when you got stabbed, (Pause) and I want you to go back to the cause of that, OK? And I want you to look back toward now, across... (Laughter) the eighteen lifetimes, and notice..."

Randy: "Damn, it's hard to hold on to anything with you around." (Laughter) (Discussion about getting a tissue)

Tad: "Change is a bitch, isn't it?"

Randy: (Laughs) "It just got warmer."

Tad: "Yeah, it did, didn't it? (Laughter) That was a big one, wasn't it?

Randy: "Yes."

Tad: "Now, one of the interesting things is, I want you to look along the eighteen succeeding lifetimes, and notice that all of the ones through the eighteen where you've actually let go, (Laughter) already, haven't you? (Laughter) Good job. You're good at this. (Laughter) Great, you're doing good. Let's just see where we are. Uh. I want you to go out in the future now, to a point five years from now, and I want you to look back toward now. And I want you to notice the moment that you're changed, and all the events that have changed in your Time Line both forward and back from five years from now. And that the future is indeed, now, far more achievable. I hesitate to use the word infinite, (Pause) but you could. Since you're more of a metaphysician than I am. (Laughter) I just do NLP. (Pause) And noticing that those changes have already been made, so that not only is success more possible now, not only is success more probable now, I have a feeling that it's something that you can't avoid, that it's going to hit you in the face pretty soon. (Laughter) Good job.

"Now, I'd like you to look just one more time. And I know that there may be parts of you that have created lots of new behaviors today, and I'd like to be sure that the new behaviors are agreeable, and that all the parts inside you are in alignment with and will support those new behaviors that we've created. And if there are parts that are questionable, or just have some, well, that think that they have some minor doubts. And what I'd like to do is (Laughter) ..."

Randy: "I'm glad this is on tape."

Tad: "So what I'd like to make sure that we do is to make sure that all the parts inside are in agreement, and that they know that if they look at their intentions, and their intentions for that, that ultimately they are in agreement with all these changes, because they know that they will achieve their intentions far more easily, now, because of the congruency and alignment that's inside of you. (Laughter) So I would task your..."

Randy: "The inside of my head is." (Laughs)

Tad: "That's right it is, and it should be, shouldn't it? And it'll keep right on being that way, won't it, until..."

Randy: "Until."

Tad: "Until you're complete with all this, aren't you? Because these things are often... create those kinds of experiences inside, and it's OK just to let them continue as long as it's appropriate to ensure your total success. Now, you know that's right, don't you? (Laughter) Good. So all the parts are in agreement, aren't they?"

Randy: "By habit, I go unnh, and something says, 'YES.'"

Tad: (To audience) So he's really OK with that, (To Randy) and I'd like to make sure that the mismatch part, uh, at this point understands that it is his duty, not just his responsibility, but his duty to continue to mismatch in such a way that will continue to totally support your success and satisfaction in ways that will contribute, because mismatching is very important as you know, because it allows us to make further distinctions, and I know that's important to your part that's in charge of that. I'd like to ask him if he would be willing to, wouldn't he, make sure that he continues to provide that same intention for you while allowing you to proceed totally unimpeded in your direction of success. (Pause) Good job. So now as you look out into the future again... (Pause)

Randy: (Nods, yes.)

Tad: "Good. That's good. Very good. Now, as you go through the rest of the day, we've made a number of changes, there may be some adjustments going on inside. Just allow them to continue, and allow your unconscious mind to continue (speeds up) to sort out those processes and things that it needs to sort out so that it continues to make these changes and allows you to be completely and absolutely, totally successful tonight. As you sleep it'll be able to do that, and you may have some, lots of weird dreams and lots going on inside your head and that's OK. And notice that the completion of the sorting out process will be done by the end of tonight, and it will be (slows down) totally possible for you to be (whisper) absolutely successful, now, won't it?"

Randy: "Thank you."

Tad: "Good job." (Applause)

10

Programming Your Future with Time Line

Over the years, as I looked at the subject of time management and goal setting, I began to realize that some people achieved their goals and some did not. I began to notice that there was a significant difference between the people who attained their goals and those who didn't. The people who got their goals, among other things, stored the goal differently, internally from those who did not.

Then, as I taught Time Line to NLP classes all over the country, I began noticing that the techniques I was teaching had an impact on people's ability to have what they wanted in the future. In fact, at a Master Practitioner Training in Los Angeles last year, fifty percent of the participants doubled their income. One tripled his. I remember asking him what happened. He told me that he had followed the process for programming his future that we did in class. Interestingly, he forgot about it until I asked about the effects of future programming at a subsequent class, at which point he told me that the event had happened exactly as he had programmed it into his future. What we have here is a way to program your future so that you achieve your goals, that what you want in the future becomes real, and undeniable to your brain.

As a first step in programming your future, decide what you want. Make sure it is something you really want. As you think of it, consider these questions and ask yourself: When you think about what you want, do you think about it in the future? Do you think about it as now? Have you taken the time to think about what you want in the future? Have you actually taken the time to write down your goals? Have you written down or have you thought out an organized plan for what you want in the future?

The clearer you can be about what you want in the future, and the more specific you are about your goal, the more achievable it becomes. In fact, there is a direct relationship between the specificity of the goal and its achievability. Once you have formulated your goal or outcome, by the way, NLP's outcome definition techniques are quite helpful in specifying your outcome.* Make sure that you haven't set as your goal or your outcome something which is a "state." (A "state" is essentially an emotional state, like "confidence" or "pride.") The reason why it is important not to set a state as an outcome is that putting a date in the future for the achievement of a state delays having it. Knowing what we know in NLP about states, we know that a state of confidence or any other state is something that you can have now, using anchoring or swish patterns. So in defining your outcome make sure that it is not a state and that it has time associated with it.

Here are some questions that you can ask yourself to assist you in clarifying your outcome.

KEYS TO AN ACHIEVABLE OUTCOME

1. **Stated in the positive** - "What specifically do I want?"
2. **Specify Present Situation** - "Where am I now?" (For this question, make sure that the picture is Associated.)
3. **Specify Outcome** - "What will I see, hear, feel, etc., when I have it?" (This means that the outcome is viewed as if it were accomplished now. Make it compelling. Then insert it in the future. Be sure that before you insert it in the future, that the picture is dissociated.)
4. **Evidence Procedure** - "How will I know when I have it?"
5. **Is it Congruently Desirable?** - "What will this outcome get for me or allow me to do?"
6. **Is it Self-Initiated and Maintained?** - "Is this only for me?"
7. **Is it Appropriately Contextualized?** - "Where, when, how and with whom do I want it?"
8. **Resources** - "What resources do I have now, and what resources do I need to get my outcome?"
   a. "Have I ever had/done this before?"
   b. "Do I know anyone else who has it?"
   c. "Just suppose I had it now."

Magic Demystified, Lewis and Pucelik, Metamorphous Press

9. **Check Ecology** - "For what purpose do I want this? What will I gain/lose if I have it?"
   a. "What will happen if I get it?"
   b. "What won't happen if I get it?"
   c. "What will happen if I don't get it?"
   d. "What won't happen if I don't get it?"

By asking these questions, you will probably have an excellent idea of what you want. I am assuming that by now you will also have a rather detailed picture of what you want.

Put that picture aside for a moment, and float up above your Time Line. If you haven't done this yet, go back and read the Time Line Therapy chapter from the beginning and then come back here after you've done the exercises there. Floating above your Time Line, float out into the future to the time when it would be most appropriate for you to have accomplished this outcome. Go out to the point in the future when you will have accomplished the desired result. When you find the most appropriate moment for the accomplishment of your outcome, position yourself above that point in your Time Line.

Now, bring up the picture of what you want, the one that you made earlier. Associate into the picture. Float right into your body, and feel the feelings of having what you want. Check your feelings as you make sure that the picture is bright enough, but not too bright. Notice the feelings you have, and increase or decrease the brightness until the feelings are the strongest. Next, bring it closer and closer until the picture is close enough so that the feelings are the most intense, but not too close. Turn up the colors so they are really, really rich, but not too rich. You know, just right! Make sure that the focus is very clear. Clear enough, but not too clear. Make any other adjustments you need to make the picture the most real and desirable. And when you're done, step out of the picture, so you see yourself in the picture, looking at yourself.

Now, staying in the future, as you put the picture in your Time Line, turn back around and look toward now. Notice that all the events between then and now are changing and rearranging themselves so as to totally support your having exactly what you want in the future. And you can, can't you?

Come back to now and, looking toward the future, notice that this is just the beginning of your having what you want. Notice that the accomplishment of this event sets a direction of accomplishment for you in the future, and that it continues out into the future as far as you can see. Notice how good it feels to have what you want.

Earlier when we asked questions about your goal, you might have noticed that you needed certain resources for the accomplishment of your outcome. (Let's suppose for purposes of this exercise that you discovered that a resource you needed was to learn about something, in order to achieve your outcome.)

So, I'd like to ask you to float back into the past to a time, a happy time, when you learned something easily and elegantly. The learning doesn't need to be something related to a school situation, just a time when you learned something easily, and perhaps so easily that you surprised yourself. You may have said, "Wow, I didn't know I knew all that," or something like that. It could be any context where you were perhaps even surprised by how easy it was to recall the information. Maybe you were talking to a friend, or to several friends, and you were pleasantly surprised about how much you knew about the subject.

(If you can't remember a time like that, then imagine what it might be like to have had that experience. Perhaps you've seen it in a movie or had a friend who had that experience. Imagine what it would be like to have it, or pretend you're someone who has had that experience.)

Good. So float right down into your body, and feel the feelings of being an exquisite learner. Now, wrap the feelings of being an excellent learner around you. Take those feelings and let them permeate your body. Feel the feelings of being a great learner. And here's one more thing. Before you had the feelings of being an excellent learner, your unconscious mind had been going through a process of allowing it to be assimilating and organizing all the information that you needed into a format that the conscious mind could easily use as it needed. Whether or not you were conscious of it, your unconscious mind was doing the work of making that information available to you in a usable way. So bring that process, even if you aren't fully conscious of it, with you as you float back up above your Time Line.

Good. Now, float back above your Time Line and float toward now, and as you approach and pass now, find the appropriate place to put all that you need to know to ensure your outcome. Take the feelings and put them in that most appropriate place, in your future. As you do, I'd like you to notice that the experience of being such a good learner changes and affects all the events between then and now, and that in the future you can draw on this strategy of being such an elegant learner any time you choose. Any time you want you can have that ability. Any time you want these learning resources they will be available to you. So, any time in the future when you need to learn something, or you need to use any information stored in your unconscious mind, it will be there for you automatically.

Turn and look toward now, and notice that the process is also installed, and that it reaches back all the way to now, and even into the past. Even if you don't notice it, that's all right, because the process is now installed all the way from now, out into the future, and even further into the future beyond the event and out into the future as far as you can see. Your ability has always been there and now you can make use of it as you need.

When you have done that, turn and float toward now, float right back into now, and then open your eyes.

This is how to program your future.

ASSOCIATED VS. DISSOCIATED

When you put a future memory back into the future, it should be dissociated. When you complete work on something you want to make compelling, make sure it's dissociated. (A memory that is associated is an outcome or a goal. A memory that is dissociated is a direction.) Dissociated future events tend to generalize better than do associated future events—rule of thumb.

The problem with reaching a goal is that the mission has been accomplished. You have it, and then what? Sometimes if a future memory is associated, you have the feeling of already having it. It's less compelling if it's associated. Dissociated is more compelling because you do not have the feelings of already having it. If you have the feelings of already having it, then you're associated.

Dissociated makes it more compelling and gives a sense of direction.

Let us examine the question of direction for a moment. A goal is something that when you reach it, you are complete. Now what? Did you ever have a goal that you really wanted? You reached it, and then you said, "Gee, now what do I do?" First you had that goal in mind and there was lots of momentum. After you reached the goal, everything seemed to change, and the momentum of going toward the goal was gone. In that case, you attained your outcome but you didn't have a direction set up beyond the outcome. If your outcome is dissociated, it creates a direction so you continue to go beyond that particular goal or event in the same direction.

It's the same rule for swish patterns—present state—associated, future desired state—dissociated. Present state associated, desired state dissociated.

11

Time Line Therapy
Outline

TIME LINE POSSIBILITIES:

There are several different possibilities for change work using Time Line Therapy. Each way will have a major effect on the personality of the individual.

1. **Memory Removal:** Take the memory out of the Time Line, and blow it up in the sun. Then replace it with a favorable memory.

2. **Change Events:** You can go in to an event and change it. Say, "Now run the movie, looking through your own eyes, acting the way you would act, with all the new resources you need." That is a standard for changing personal history. But then you can also have them change the gestalt, saying, "... so notice how changing this event also changes other events forward and back on the Time Line that are of a similar nature." They will go through and make the changes.

3. **Delete Negative Emotions:** You can erase negative emotions such as guilt, shame, anxiety and fear. The procedure is to float people above their Time Line, and have them go 15 minutes on the other side of the event about which they had the negative emotion. Then have them look toward now, and say, "Now, where's the emotion?" The emotion will disappear. Alternately you can unhook the emotions (a metaphor) from the lower right hand corner (lower left hand if they're reverse organized) and then have them step

out of the picture—step out, so they can see themselves in the picture. This will dissociate them from their feelings.

4. **Phobia Model:** What does the Phobia Model do? The Phobia Model, if you run it enough times, will destroy the memory. In this model, run a movie of the memory dissociated in black and white, at high speed out to the point of maximum emotion or to the end, freeze-frame and white-out or black-out. Then out of the white-out turn the brightness back down (dim the brightness until they can see the picture), associate to it and run it backwards in color. That's the Phobia Model. If you run it enough, it will destroy the memory. You can also assist it by giving the appropriate suggestions.

   The most I've ever had to run the phobia model is 15 times. This was on a very intense phobia. When we had run it 15 times, the memory was destroyed. The Phobia Model begins by blurring the distinctions during the initial three or four times it runs. This causes the person to have a lot less feeling with the memory. After three or four times, they may still have the memory, but it will be fuzzier or less distinct.

5. **Compelling Future:** There are ways in Time Line Therapy to change the future to make it more compelling. I don't know of any reasons to want to make a memory more compelling. You can change future events to make them more compelling. (See "Programming your Future on Time Line.")

6. **Changing the Direction of the Time Line:** Finally, you can change the way people organize time by changing them from In Time to Through Time or vice versa. Just have them float above their Time Line, and then say, "Now, as you float back down into now, just rotate your Time Line by 90 degrees so that:

   a. it is all in front of you and stretches from right to left, or

   b. your past is behind you."

This will change a person from In Time to Through Time, or vice versa.

SAMPLE OUTLINE OF TIME LINE THERAPY USING GESTALTS

Time Line Therapy is an especially fast and effective means for producing changes that relate to memory (past and future), including changing an individual's personal history, and is especially fast and effective in changing the chain of events that created a certain set of unwanted behaviors or internal states.

1. **Discover if the person is In Time or Through Time.**
2. **Have them Float above their Time Line.**
3. **Note the Submodalities, and make sure that the client's experience is that SMds are the same for the past, present and future.** If not the same, change the SMds so that they are the same brightness, and approximate color, or the future slightly brighter than the past.
4. **Have them go back into the past and find the earliest unwanted experience in the chain that they can find.** (If using a visual squash, such as Robert Dilts' model for integration, have the new part do it.)
5. **Have them preserve the learnings,** saying, "Just before we change these memories, I want you to preserve these learnings in the special place that you reserve for your learnings."
6. **Change the memory using the Guilt/Anxiety Model, Change Personal History, or Phobia Model, or just have them remove the memory.** If you are using the Phobia Model, ask them to run the pattern until the memory is destroyed. Say, "I want you to run it until you can't get the memory back."
7. If you removed any memories, **replace the removed memories** with favorable ones using swish patterns or movies.
8. **Continue steps 4-6** using the earliest memory available, until the unwanted memory, state or behavior is not accessible.
9. **Have them float down back into their time line and come to now.**
10. **Future Pace and Test...** (Have them go out in the future and look back to now. Test ecology.)

III

Meta Programs

12

Introduction To
Meta Programs

Meta Programs are the most unconscious filters to our perception. Unlike our memories, which can be either conscious or unconscious, Meta Programs are wholly unconscious. Even so, they are powerful determinants of personality. Carl Jung* thought that he could predict which of sixteen personality types a person was simply by knowing four of the most basic Meta Programs.

SUMMARY

We have been using Meta Programs to measure and predict behavior in a business context for a number of years. During that time, we developed a complete profiling system, which is in use by all the Profitability Consulting offices throughout the United States. The Meta Programs and Values Inventory™, MPVI™ analysis is a model that will allow you to quickly determine the thought processes of your client or colleague and therefore to predict his behavior or actions. The MPVI™ can be elicited in an interview that can take less than a half hour. (The form is available at no charge from the author. Write to the address at the front of this book.) With the MPVI™, you have a reasonable system for predicting a person's actions. The MPVI™ is explained fully in this chapter; the next two chapters will illustrate and explain each category.

THE MPVI™

You will remember that we create our internal representations of the events in our lives by filtering the information that comes

---

Psychological Types, Carl Jung, Princeton University Press, 1971)

in through our five senses. The process of filtering distorts, deletes and generalizes the information so that we do not exceed the seven (plus or minus two) chunks of information available to our conscious minds.* How we filter is a result of Meta Programs, Values, Beliefs, Decisions and Memories.

THE MODEL OF COMMUNICATION

The MPVI™ is part of a model of communication that includes both internal (self-talk) and external communication. We distort, delete and generalize information because the conscious mind can only pay attention to so many pieces of information at any given time. Meta Programs and values determine how we look at the world, and determine how we distort, delete and generalize the information that comes in through our senses, as well as how we access our archival memory and what we focus on when we access it. They are just one of the filters that we use.

FILTERS

Meta Programs are one of the internal programs or filters that we unconsciously use in determining what to pay attention to. (Sometimes Meta Program categories are called "sorting" categories. "Sort" is a term used in computers, which essentially describes how the computer has organized certain information.) They are how we formulate, maintain or break generalizations through time. They are how we create generalizations, establish a sense of coherence and maintain it through time. Meta Programs give quality to our experience, and they are the patterns that determine our interest and attention. They give our experience continuity, and are one of the basic building blocks that make up our personality. They are deeply buried in our unconscious. Meta Programs are categories that describe internal patterns, and like all NLP patterns, they change over time and from context to context. Our use of Meta Programs is the result of our emotional state at the time. That is, their use can be different according to the state of the individual, the context in which he is active and according to the amount of stress that a person is experiencing.

---

*"The Magic Number 7 Plus or Minus 2", G. A. Miller, in the *American Psychologist*, 1956.

People may use Meta Programs differently in a resourceful state and an unresourceful state. They are also culturally independent, although the percentages of people in a certain category (as in the Relationship Filter) may differ from culture to culture.

PREDICTION AND CAVEATS

Knowing someone's Meta Programs can help you closely predict his actions, and we offer these categories with the caveat that there is no one "right" way to be or to filter information. The use of one pattern is not right and another wrong. Some patterns are more useful in a certain context than others. The model therefore has usefulness. The Meta Programs are not presented here for the purpose of allowing you, the reader, to be able to put people in little boxes. We resist that. Use them to make people's lives, including your own, better.

It's also important to make a critical distinction about behavior: People are NOT their behaviors. People HAVE behaviors, and we believe that they always do the best they can with the resources they have available. People have inside them all the resources they need to make changes that they want to make. All they need is new information or different strategies to assist them in making the change. Just because you "screw up" doesn't mean you ARE a "screw up." We can change that. Using this model, we can assist someone in changing and improving his Meta Programs.

Remember also that the highest quality information is behavioral. That means that as you ask the questions to determine a person's Meta Programs, also observe your client's behavior. Note if it contradicts his spoken answer. If there is a contradiction, rely on the non-verbal behavior. After you have a premise about someone, keep on re-evaluating. Even though you know their Meta Programs, you can still keep looking.

The complex Meta Programs were originally developed by Richard Bandler, and later expanded by Rodger Bailey.

13

The Simple Meta
Programs

THE FOUR BASIC META PROGRAMS

Sigmund Freud was one of the people in the history of psychology who was concerned with defining the elements that make up the basis of personality. Freud had two primary students—Jung and Adler. The basis of Meta Programs is based largely on Carl Jung's work as outlined in his book *Psychological Types*, written in 1923. Jung was concerned with type casting a person in order to predict his personality and therefore his behavior. Jung's work was later continued by Isabel Briggs Myers, who used it in creating the Myers-Briggs Type Indicator, the most widely used psychological profiling system in business and government today.

In each case, the desire was to discover what elements make up a person's personality. Interestingly enough, Jung's and Myers' models fit quite nicely into the NLP model. In fact, it seems that their work is completely aligned with the model of personality in NLP.

In NLP, we are concerned with Internal Processes, Internal States and External Behaviors:

Internal Processes are the internal processing strategies that we use, essentially the "how"—*how* we do what we do. Internal States are the emotional states that an individual experiences, providing the "why"—why we do what we do. External Behavior is the "what"—what is generated as a result of the combination of the Internal Processes and the Internal States. This model

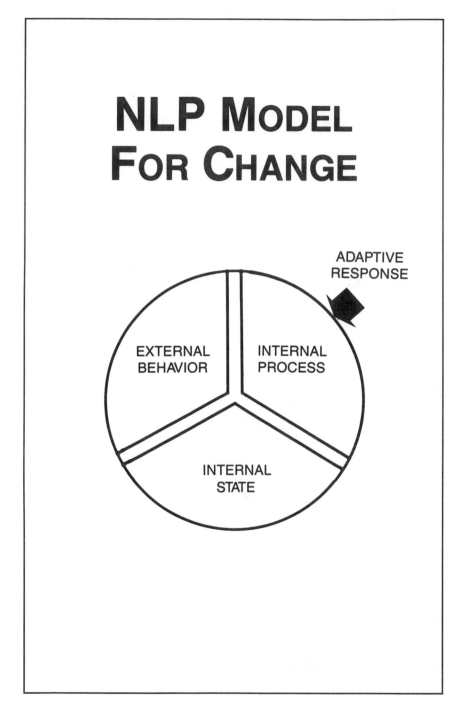

is essentially the same as the model presented in the Introduction (page 3). It is just another way of looking at it. These are essentially the domain of what we work on in NLP. We change a person's External Behavior by changing his physiology. We change his Internal Processes through working with strategies. Internal States are influenced by changing the filters and by anchoring. Our model contains one additional distinction—people are influenced by their storage of time, which in turn determines whether they will adapt to change easily or will resist change. We call this the Adaptive Response, which is the "what if"—what if something happens, and what if it does not.

Interestingly enough, the first three elements correspond directly to the distinctions regarding personality in Jung's work—Introvert/Extravert, Sensor/Intuitor, and Thinker/Feeler. The fourth element is implied by Jung's work, and appears in Isabel Briggs Myers' work as the Judger/Perceiver preference. These filtering processes form four simple Meta Programs. It is also possible that these four Basic Meta Programs form the other 16-24 Complex Meta Programs through their interaction. Although this assumption is as yet unproven, we have discovered that certain of the Complex Meta Programs are indeed formed by the interaction of two or three or four of the simple Meta Programs. Knowing these basic filters can therefore give you a basis for changing the Complex Meta Programs.

A preference for any one of the categories (category in this context means, for example, the categories of Introvert/Extravert in the External Behavior Meta Program) in each of the four Simple Meta Programs presented below is just that, a preference. We often move through the full range of each of the categories of the Meta Programs described as we go through our day. We also use these filters differently in different contexts. So using just one question to elicit these basic Meta Programs may not be as accurate for determining a person's preference as a greater number would be. The Myers Briggs, for example, uses roughly 25 questions to determine each of the four preferences, and it is certainly more accurate.

1. EXTERNAL BEHAVIOR: Introvert/Extravert

External Behavior is determined by the basic question of whether a person is an Introvert or an Extravert. This was described by Jung as an attitude preference. The question answered by this description is, "What is your attitude toward the external world that is evidenced by your behavior?" As measured in the Myers-Briggs Type Indicator, there are roughly 25 questions that are used to determine whether a person is an Introvert or an Extravert. Of course, asking 25 questions may be more accurate than asking one, so you will also want to observe the person's behavior after you've made a postulation of who they are.

QUESTION:

"When it's time to recharge your batteries, do you prefer to be alone or with people?"

A) Introvert:

Someone who is introverted will prefer to be alone; he prefers the internal world of thoughts and ideas over the external world of people and things. Asking the above question will usually separate the Introvert from the Extravert. Although some Introverts can learn to come out of their shells and do well with other people, when it comes to the question of recharging their batteries, they prefer to be alone.

Introverts make up roughly 25% of the population. As an Introvert, a person will be more interested in the inner world of concepts and ideas than in the outer world of actions, objects and people. He will be more interested in how that idea, person or thing influences their beliefs. He will have a greater depth of concentration (as opposed to breadth of interest). Introverts will view Extraverts as shallow and not real or genuine. Introverts will have a certain space or territory that they call their own. An Introvert will be "lonely in a crowd." Even at a party an Introvert can be lonely. (Whereas an Extravert says, "Look at all these people. How can you be lonely?")

Introverts tend to
   have few friends and look for deeper relations with them
   look to self for causes
   reflect before acting   be self sufficient
   enjoy working alone   be less carefree
   be more solitarys   value aesthetics

score highly on aptitude test
like to deal with concepts and ideas

Introverts tend to prefer jobs like:

mathematician	engineer
dentist	artist
writer	printer
farmer	carpenter
technical jobs	creative architect
scientific jobs	creative research scientist

B) Extravert:

An Extravert will prefer the outer world of people and things rather than the internal world of thoughts and ideas. When it is time to recharge their batteries, Extraverts will want to be with people.

Extraverts make up most of the people in the United States. They are 75% of the population. An Extravert will be more interested in the outer world of actions, objects and persons than the inner world of concepts and ideas. They will be more interested in how the idea, person or thing impacts others. Extraverts will have a greater breadth of interest (as opposed to depth of concentration). They prefer interaction with other people and a breadth of friendships. Extraverts are into interaction, while Introverts prefer concentration.

Extraverts tend to:

have many friends, and not deep relations with them
be sociable

look to the environment for causes	be stable
be happy-go-lucky	be venturesome
like action	be talkative
get involved in new situations	be gregarious
be impulsive	be outgoing
show social adjustment	have ego strength
like interaction	

Extraverts tend to prefer jobs like:

salesperson	personnel director
social worker	public
athletic director	administrator

Some of the complex Meta Programs directly related to the External Behavior category of Introvert/Extravert are Attention Direction and Frame of Reference. To a lesser extent Action Level, Work Style and Primary Filter are also related to this basic filter.

2. INTERNAL PROCESSES: Intuitor/Sensor

Internal Processes or strategies are directly related to our level of attention and where we focus it. As written in *NLP Volume I*, all of the four tuple <V,A,K,O,G> (Visual, Auditory, Kinesthetic, Olfactory, Gustatory) are going on even though a person may at a given moment favor just one of them. Therefore (and we admit it may be a stretch) the level of attention is based on how a person "chunks" in the range from abstract to specific. (See "Hierarchy of Ideas", page 193.) It works like this: In a specific strategy, the predominant modality favored at any given moment is based on where you place your attention. Since each modality (Visual, Auditory, Kinesthetic, etc.) carries varying amounts of information, our internal processes are determined by the level of chunking. When the Myers-Briggs Type Indicator tests for Sensor/Intuitor they are testing for chunk size.

That leads us to the question:

"If you were going to study a certain subject, would you be more interested solely in the facts and their application for the now, or would you be more interested in the ideas and relationships between the facts and their application for the future?"

A) Intuitor:

An Intuitor will prefer to perceive the possibilities, the relationships and the meaning of their experiences (as opposed to immediate facts and experiences themselves). Intuitors make up only 25% of the population. They will be more interested in the abstract big picture as opposed to the specific details. The Intuitor is most interested in the future, and in grasping possibilities. The Intuitor is so much into relationships that he may disregard sensory data coming in right now. They may disregard it to the point that they fail to notice what is going on now. Intuitors describe themselves as imaginative and ingenious, and the Sensor as being too much of a "stick-in-the-mud."

Intuitors tend to:
>   have a positive attitude toward change
>   like new possibilities
>   be tolerant of complexity
>   be aesthetic and theoretical
>   like open ended instructions
>   value autonomy
>   seek patterns in complex situations
>   prefer working at symbolic and abstract levels
>   be more creative in direct proportion to their Intuitor score
>   have higher turnover in mechanical/clerical jobs
>   read more for pleasure than Sensors

Intuitors tend to prefer jobs like:

research scientist	architect
writer	mathematician
psychologist	musician
minister	physicist
chemist	

Regarding time, Intuitors will be the poets, dreamers and visionaries. They are the dreamers. They dream of a world that they would like to have in the future, and then they move toward that dream. They are constantly trying to make today into what they already envision for tomorrow. This kind of inspiration for the future is often lacking for the Sensor, who is mostly in the now. Intuitors, however, have no patience for doing the actual work of "getting there," because they are still farther off in the future and dreaming up new plans.

And what is intuition? It is simply the ability to (1) move to levels of greater abstraction of thinking, (2) find the relationships between ideas and then (3) move to levels of greater specificity or more detailed thinking and (4) relate it to the current situation. This is the process. Of course, some intuitions make sense, others do not. You may have noticed that some Intuitors make no sense at all or, if they do, the message is buried deep in your contemplation of it.

Have you ever read Marshall McLuhan, by the way? I read McLuhan back in the '60s. He was considered one of the world's foremost communication theorists, and coined the phrase, "the medium is the message." Reading McLuhan was really deep. I would read one sentence and then go away and think about it for a year. That's an Intuitor! Buckminster Fuller is another Intuitor. After reading his writings, you have to go into outer space and think for a while! To say the least, they both wrote very abstractly. The dividing line between Intuitor and the Sensor, which is the more detailed or specific of the two, has to do with, "Are they writing (speaking or thinking) abstractly or specifically?"

B) Sensor:

Sensors are in the majority (as are Extraverts), making up 75% of the population. A Sensor prefers to perceive the immediate, real, practical facts of experience and life (as opposed to the relationships between the ideas). They will be more interested in the concrete as opposed to the abstract. The Sensor relies on facts and is most interested in experiencing the "now." In fact, the Sensor is so much into the sense experience of the now that he tends to disregard "hunches." Sensors think they are realistic and down-to-earth. They call Intuitors speculative and think that Intuitors have their heads in the clouds. (The average American businessman is a Sensor, the average NLP Practitioner is an intuitor. This accounts for the problems in communication between NLP people and business.)

Sensors tend to:
    be factual minded   be solid and realistic
    learn through visual aids   need order
    be interested in economics   be shrewd
    value authority and work   learn through visual aids
    prefer practical applications
    have a practical outlook
    in mechanical jobs Sensors stay longer than Intuitors
    be willing to take directions that proceed toward defined
        goals

Sensors tend to prefer jobs like:

business	administration
production	sales
biological science	technology
office management	banking
veterinary medicine	farming
police work	

Regarding time, Sensors are in the now. They often have short memories and not much ability to look toward the future. Some are notoriously poor planners. Since they are caught up in the "now," they are usually concerned with the events in the moment. They can be quick decision makers, and they are able to respond to events that are going on. Often energetic and active, Sensors want stimulating experiences in the now.

Intelligence tests that are currently in use in the United States tend to be biased toward Intuitors, since a Sensor needs to weigh all of the answers for a specific question in the test, while an Intuitor can often see at a glance which is the right answer. So on the Myers-Briggs, there tends to be a direct correlation between the score of the individual on the Intuitor scale and his level of intelligence.

A number of the complex Meta Programs are related to Internal Process: Chunk Size, Relationship and Direction, among others.

3. INTERNAL STATE: Thinker (Dissociated)/Feeler (Associated)

The ability to access a certain Internal State is based on the question of whether the person is associated or dissociated. Remember that when you're assisting a person in accessing a certain state, he needs to be associated. When assisting someone in accessing a fully associated state it is useful to say, "Can you remember a time when you were motivated (or some other state that you want them to access)? Can you remember a specific time? As you remember that time, can you step into your body and see what you saw, hear what you heard and what you said to yourself, and feel the feelings of being motivated?"

This sort of language allows your client to go more easily into a specific state, because he becomes associated. (When considering a picture, it means looking through your own eyes.) So the key to having a person go into a specific state is having him associate. Some people find it easy to go into state (they prefer to be associated) and some find it not so easy (they prefer to be dissociated). The Internal State is therefore a function of whether a person is associated or dissociated. This function changes often and with context. Over time, however, a person will come to favor Associated or Dissociated as a primary mode of operation. People who tend to favor Auditory Digital tend to be more dissociated and are called Thinkers. People who tend to favor Kinesthetic (Internal) tend to be more associated and are called Feelers. (This particular Meta Program is not concerned with which Representational System a person prefers.)

QUESTION:

Although the Myers-Briggs uses about 25 questions to determine this filter, you can use any one of three questions to get a rough sketch. (1) **"Can you remember a work situation that gave you trouble (a one-time event)?"** (2) **"Can you remember a work situation in which you were the happiest?"** If you use either question 1 or 2, after you ask the question, notice if your client accesses the Kinesthetic (with his eyes). The duration of Kinesthetic accessing will indicate the amplitude of Feeling on a Thinking (Dissociated)—Feeling (Associated) scale. (Once you have determined Thinking or Feeling, it is also interesting to notice which of your client's good memories or bad memories are associated or dissociated.) Alternately you can use another question: (3) **"When you make a decision do you rely more on impersonal reason and logic, or more on personal values?"**

A) Thinkers:

Thinkers are Dissociated, and make up 50% of the population. (Forty-five per cent of all women and 55% of men are Thinkers.) A Thinker will make judgments or decisions objectively and impersonally, considering both the causes of events and where decisions may lead. They will make judgments based on criteria, and in an impersonal way. They believe in principles, policies and laws. The Thinker, being a rational person, will not take into account how decisions may matter to others. The Thinker is "atemporal," meaning that time often does not matter to the Thinker. The "rational thinking man" is the source of Western science. This is the basis of the Xerox Sales Training system, which assumes that man is a rational being. Xerox believes that all decisions are made rationally and logically.

Thinkers tend to:
  be skeptical of religious orthodoxy
  have a theoretical orientation
  excel in mechanical aptitude
  be experimental
  learn best from lectures
  do well on exams
  need order, autonomy, dominance, achievement,
    endurance

Thinkers tend to prefer jobs like:

law	politics
physical and biological sciences	mechanical jobs
medicine	dentistry
business	related technologies

When it comes to time, Thinkers perceive time as objective fact, but it is outside of themselves. Thinkers therefore can be more abstract in their thinking about time. They do, however, have respect for time. They view it in a dissociated way as the whole continuum of past/present/future (atemporal) in which events are analyzed as impersonal, historical situations. To a Thinker, "what happened when" is more important than "why" it happened. They are usually comfortable with facts and they may be uncomfortable when asked to speculate.

B) Feelers:

Feelers comprise 50% of the population. (Forty-five per cent of all men are Feelers, and 55% of women are Feelers.) A Feeler will make judgments or decisions subjectively and personally, weighing the value of choices based on their "past" and on how these values matter to others. As an irrational person the Feeler may not care about logic. The Wilson Learning System (sales training) believes that all decisions are made emotionally and non-logically.

Feelers tend to:
   be more social
   be more religious
   be into nurturing, affiliating
   have more free-floating anxiety
   be more tender-minded

Feelers tend to prefer jobs like:

social services	nursing
customer relations	ministry
teaching	counseling

Feelers are associated with the past, and they take time personally. They are impressed with the events of the past, and may think that the past is somehow more real than the present or the future. They may even wish to have lived in the past. The future is not real to them, since neither they nor anyone they know has lived through it. The past and the present are the only reality for them. The feeler will tell you: "This reminds me of a time..." as he relates the past to the present. Metaphors are often more effective with a feeler (especially if you relate them to the past).

To change someone from a feeler to a thinker, just dissociate them in the context or situation. To change a person from a thinker to a feeler, just associate them in the context or situation. Anchoring and swish patterns will be the most effective in making this change.

4. THE ADAPTIVE RESPONSE: Judger/Perceiver

The adaptive response determines how people adapt to their environment. Does a person go through life aiming to understand life and adapt to it, or in a decisive, planned and orderly way that aims to regulate and control events? Myers-Briggs says that this filter is the basis of whether a person is aiming to experience life and adapt to it, or make life adapt to them. A Judger will have plans and lists, and will have decided in advance how it should be. A Judger needs high closure. A Perceiver tends to adapt more and stay away from closure. (This is quite similar to the Options/ Procedures sort as taught by some NLP trainers. It is not, however, the Reason sort.)

QUESTION:

There tends to be a high degree of correlation between In Time and Perceiver, and between Through Time and Judger (see Time Line), so any question that you might use to determine In Time or Through Time will help you determine: Judger or Perceiver. Determining this correlation using Time Line elicitation techniques takes considerable precision. However, there are a number of other questions that you can use to determine this filter: (1) **"If we were going to do a project together, would you prefer that it were outlined, planned and orderly or would you prefer that we were able to be more flexible in the project?"** (2) **"Do you have a Daytimer type calendar? Do you use it regularly? Do you enjoy using it?"** (3) **"Why** (not how) **did you buy your last car?"** (A Judger will give you a list of chronological events that led to the purchase. A Perceiver will give you a list of criteria or values.)

A) Judgers:

Judgers make up 50% of the population. A Judger wants to run his own life and prefers to live in a decisive, planned and orderly way. They aim to regulate and control events. The Judger wants to know what is going to happen a week from Wednesday. They like to have things "settled" (that's actually a good word for a judger—"settled"). Indeed, they may plan to the minute for months or even years in advance. They may, therefore, react poorly in situations where they have no plan. Since they have a high need for closure, they may experience anxiety around not deciding. If you tell a Judger, "I want to tell you four things,

1, 2, 3..." and leave out the fourth, he will experience anxiety about not knowing the fourth. The Judger also likes to make lists and to be organized. They are the people who carry those little time management books, and they love them!

Judgers tend to:
   be decisive
   have vocational interests
   be quicker at decision making
   like using administrative skills
   be "left-brained"

Judgers tend to prefer jobs like:
   business oriented professions   executive
   school principal   police officer

The Judger tends to favor Thinking or Feeling as the primary process in experiencing the external world.

B) Perceivers:

Half the population are Perceivers. A Perceiver wants to let his life happen, and will prefer to live life in a spontaneous, flexible way. They aim to understand life and adapt to it. The perceiver says: "Take it as it comes." They like the open-endedness of not having made a decision yet. They don't like lists. They don't like schedules or deadlines, because they have a high need to keep their options open. They experience anxiety around deciding, since the decision may reduce their options. In studying a subject they want to read just one more book and get that one last fact in. The Perceiver may even be reading three or four books simultaneously without completing one of them.

I have a friend in Honolulu who is really high on the Judger scale on the Myers-Briggs Type Indicator. For Christmas, he gave his wife, who is a high percciver, a time management book, as if that would do it. She threw it in the closet and won't have anything to do with it. (And who could blame her? Certainly not a Perceiver.)

Perceivers tend to:
   be open to change   be spontaneous
   be flexible   be open-minded
   be impulsive   need change
   perform below capacity   need autonomy

be less competitive than Judgers
have a high tolerance for complexity
be better at abstract reasoning
be right brained

Perceivers tend to prefer jobs like:

writer	artist
musician	psychologist
architect	advertising

The Perceiver tends to favor Sensing or Intuition as his primary way of experiencing the external world.

These Basic Meta Programs are preferences. Understand that people move through the range of each of the categories all the time. It's important, therefore, to continually observe, observe, and observe.

Changing these preferences is quite possible and in many cases relatively easy. See "Changing Meta Programs" in this section.

14

Complex Meta Programs

The Complex Meta Programs below are in the same order as on the MPVI™ questionnaire, designed for easy conversational elicitation, and are not listed in the order of importance. We feel that the most important of these complex filters involved in predicting how a person will act and react are the Relationship Sort, Direction Sort, Attention Direction and Frame of Reference Sort. Each of the Meta Programs is distinct—the answer to one filter will not necessarily affect another.

When the Complex Meta Programs were first developed, they were extracted through observation during conversation with the client. They were not elicited through specific questions, however, and the preferences were expected to "appear" in a conversation of an hour or more. In business and personnel evaluation for hiring, of course, this may be a little too much time to spend in typing a person. Our desire, and we believe our contribution, in organizing these Complex Meta Programs, was to allow for an interview of ten minutes or less to elicit roughly 20 Meta Programs, using these questions for elicitation. Our experience has shown us that the use of these questions can be equally effective or even more effective than the original mode of Meta Program elicitation. In addition, these questions will substantially reduce the time needed to discover the Meta Programs. As you ask the questions, remember that you are looking for information about process and not content.

A number of states have recently outlawed the use of paper and pencil instruments in hiring and classifying employees for placement. If this unfortunate trend continues, the MPVI will continue to be appropriate and (of course) legal, in that it is simply "interviewing skills training." It is important, therefore, as you elicit a person's Meta Programs, to be sure to ask the questions in a way that is non-judgmental, and in which your tone of voice is neutral and does not bias the answers.

PART OF A CONTINUUM

For the most part, unless otherwise noted, the categories in each Meta Program are part of a continuum, and not necessarily either-or. So, as you elicit someone's Meta Programs, you may discover that the person is not one or the other but a little of both.

Meta Programs are important in modeling patterns of excellence, hiring and screening applicants, and team-building applications.

1. DIRECTION FILTER

Every human either moves toward or away from. The Direction Filter has to do with your values and what's important to you. It deals with whether you move toward or away from these values and whether you have an approach (attraction, reward) or avoidance (repulsion, punishment) type of personality. Here in the Direction Filter, Meta Programs and Values meet and interact.

In eliciting this filter, we are looking for the PREDOMINANT direction, the way a person responds most of the time in most situations. (Remember that Meta Programs may vary according to state, context and stress levels.) In addition, it's important to note that at some level almost everyone will move away from.

When you ask someone what he wants in life, he will either tell you what he wants or what he doesn't want. **"Toward" people move toward what they like. "Away from" people move away from what they don't like.**

QUESTIONS: (The Direction Filter is usually elicited in a specific context.)

> **"What do you want in a job?" "What do you want in a relationship?" "What do you want in a car?" "What do you want to do with your life?" "What's important about what you do?"**

In answering this question, your client will either tell you what he wants or what he doesn't want. Toward answers will be about what a person wants. Away from answers will be about what a person does not want. When you elicit this Meta Program, you will find that a number of the words your client gives you are Nominalizations. (A nominalization is a process word that has been turned into a noun, like communication, relationship, freedom. The test for a nominalization is, "Can you put it into a wheelbarrow?" If "yes," then the word is not a Nominalization.) The Nominalizations you hear are the client's values. The values you hear will be either toward or away fom, or may imply both Toward and Away From, so you may want to ask the person for the meaning, the complex equivalents for the information that has just been given to you. For example, if the answer is "money," then say, "What does money get you?" or, "What will having that do for you?"

A) Toward

Toward people move toward what they like. Away from people move away from what they don't like. A toward person is motivated by his desires, so to motivate them, give them a goal or reward or "carrot" to move toward.

To motivate a toward person, give them a "carrot," not a stick. If you try to motivate a toward person with a "stick," you'll only get him angry. In sales, someone who moves toward will want to know the benefits and enjoyment, how sales will increase, or how much more fun the product will produce. In business, perks and benefits will motivate the toward person, harsh disciplinary measures will not.

B) Toward with a little Away From

A toward person with a little away from is motivated primarily by what he wants, but is also motivated away from what he wants to avoid. This kind of person has a desire to move toward what he wants but will also, to a certain extent, take into account the negative consequences of what could go wrong in the situation.

C) Both Toward and Away From Equally

Someone who is motivated equally toward and away from is motivated by what he wants, but is also motivated by what he wants to avoid. He moves toward what he wants, but will equally take into account the negative consequences of what could go wrong.

D) Away From with a little Toward

The away from with a little toward person is motivated primarily by what he wants to avoid. They take into account negative consequences and identify what could go wrong, while having a lesser desire to achieve.

E) Away From

Away from people move away from what they don't like. (Toward people move toward what they like.) They are often best motivated by their fears. To motivate those who move away from, give them something big and negative to move away from, like getting fired! If you try to motivate away from people with a "carrot," they won't care. In sales, someone who moves away from will want to cut costs and repairs, cut down-time and avoid failure. In business, perks and benefits will not motivate the away from person; he will probably want a raise now BECAUSE he needs to pay some past-due bills. The away from person will respond better to not being put in certain situations that he doesn't want to be in. This type of person often chooses a job because the job is not as bad as being somewhere else!

OTHER PATTERNS

There are other variations of toward and away from patterns, and it's valuable to notice inverse patterns—someone who is moving toward too strongly may in reality be moving away from. In this case, you may want to elicit the nature of the experiences that created the desire to move toward or away from.

In the process of building a team, it is critical to understand where each player is going, toward or away from! It is important, in developing motivational processes or material, to provide something for both toward and away from people.

FURTHER DISTINCTIONS

There are several other questions that you can ask that will give you further distinctions, and while they are not included in the questionnaire, you may want to notice them as you elicit the answers to this question:

OBJECT

What is the nature of the object that they move toward or away from? Is it one of the Primary Interest Filters? (See Primary Interest Filter, page 125.)

INTENSITY

These are the sub-filters that have to do with the *intensity* of movement toward or away from. The intensity of movement is also called "motivation." These filters are critical to marketing. In this filter, you will want to discover if the person is:

A) Satisfied—they are satisfied with where they are, and do not see the importance in movement.

B) Apathetic—they are apathetic about moving toward or away from.

C) Active—they are active in their movement toward or away from, probably not satisfied. They are the go-getters.

D) Inactive—They don't care and don't do.

DEGREE

What is the degree of movement toward or away from? There are those things that you:

A) Can't not do

B) Want to do

C) Congruently desire (in alignment with your self-concept)

D) Want over the long term

E) Must do or must have

One of the goals of yoga is to overcome attractions and repulsions. Many of us find it impossible to deal with being denied our attractions. More of us would find it harder to live with our repulsions. Zen says, "The Great Way is not difficult for those who have no preferences."

AGAINST

There is a variation of the Direction Filter that is primarily operative in relationships:

A) Toward: The person who moves toward certain values or toward another person in a relationship.

B) Away From: The person who moves away from certain values or away from another person in a relationship.

C) Against: Some people move toward or away from so as to be moving against the other person or against certain values in the relationship.

2. REASON (OR MODAL OPERATOR) FILTER

The Reason Filter will tell you if a person acts as though he has choice in his life. This means it will tell you why somebody does something or is doing something. It is a strong motivational filter and will indicate if the person is motivated by possibilities in life or by obligations. The Reason Filter may also be detected by a person's use of Modal Operators (words that speak of possibility or necessity, i.e., can, can't, should). There is another complex Meta Program that is based on this one—the Modal Operator Sequence.

QUESTION

Why did you choose your present job? Why are you choosing to do what you're doing?

As you listen to the answer to this question, notice if your client gives you a reason. If there is no reason, then you're dealing with a necessity person. A reason will relate to possibilities. If someone cannot think of why he is doing it, it could be because he simply is doing what he has to do. In business, a balance is desirable.

A) Possibility

They do what they want to do. They have a reason for doing what they want to do. They will look for new opportunities, expanding options, ways and possibilities. This person believes that he has control over his life. As a result, these people are motivated to make choices in life, and to search for new ways of doing things. In fact they may see too many possibilities. They are interested in what might be—the potential. Some people in this category are not at all motivated by obligations or responsibilities.

B) Necessity

Life is a routine. There is no choice. These people sometimes can be stuck, because they have a limited model of the world, and because they often only do what needs to be done. They seldom try to find reasons for doing things since they see obligations, known options or ways, responsibilities, rules, pressures. Their action is determined by their obligations.

C) Both

The person who is both motivated by possibility and necessity will be motivated equally by having options and by having obligations. These people are motivated to seek possibilities, and yet need to fulfill their obligations, too. Although they are motivated by their obligations, they will also search for new possibilities.

3. FRAME OF REFERENCE FILTER

The Frame of Reference filter relates to how people judge the results of their actions—how they are doing (on a job, for example). Do they know inside themselves, or do they go out and check, or do they do both? Unfortunately, this filter and the Attention Direction Filter (how you show someone else you're paying attention to them) are often confused. *This* filter is about the locus of judgment. Where does a person place the judgment for his actions - inside or outside; from where does a person gather the data for making a judgment on the responsibility for his actions?

QUESTION

"**How do you know when you've done a good job?**" (Possible follow-up question: "**Do you just know inside, or does some-one have to tell you?**") The answer will either indicate that they know "inside," or that they go outside to gather data.

A) Internal Frame of Reference

"I just know," or "I had a feeling." They go inside for data to evaluate how they are doing. A person with an internal frame will know if he has done a good job based on his own internal reference system. A typical entrepreneur will have a totally internal frame of reference, and will be motivated by what *he* thinks. While good in an entrepreneurial setting, this person may be hard to manage if he is not aligned with or if he does not agree with you. In sales, if the client has an Internal Frame of Refer-ence, you would need to find out what is important to him, and then align with those criteria, describing your product or service in terms of those criteria. You might then say, "Only you will know if this is right for you."

B) External Frame of Reference

"Someone has to tell me," "I look at the figures," or "I got a reward." They go outside for data to evaluate.

An external frame person will want to know what others think about him, or what everybody else did. Entertainers often have an external frame of reference. In sales, you could tell them about all the other people who were satisfied with the product. A person with an external frame of reference will be easier to manage. You can withhold or give approval to motivate them. This person, however, may need constant praise, support and evaluation, while a balanced person will need less.

With an External Frame, you will also want to know who or what your client is using as a reference. Who specifically tells them? Are they using a specific authority, or is it a more general "they" or "people." If the external reference is not someone, then it will be something. You will then want to know if it is informa-tion or data—what specifically is the evidence procedure? It might be interesting to ask, "Who is responsible for the quality of your work?"

C) Balanced

A combination of both. They want to have an internal knowing and also like external acknowledgment or need external verification equally.

D) Internal with an External Check

A person who is Internal with an External Check will have an internal knowing, and then desire an external check. (It is also possible for this type to have a second internal knowing after the external check.) These people may, if the external data is inconsistent with their internal knowing, change their evaluation of the situation. In the absence of any external input they are satisfied with their internal evaluation.

E) External with an Internal Check

Although less important, it is also possible for a person with an External Frame to need an Internal Check. This person may be able to know if he has done a good job even in the absence of external feedback.

MATURING

The process of maturing concerns the change of Frame of Reference from external (youth) to more internal (adult). In the process of learning, we need to have an external frame of reference simply to know if we are learning what we are supposed to learn. If the frame is too strongly internal in learning, the person will not know if he is learning appropriately, or may attain premature closure on a subject. The teenage years are when an internal frame develops. Or alternatly, a teen with an external frame may change the reference from parents to peer group.

A GOAL IN NLP

One of the goals in NLP is to allow people to develop a balanced frame of reference. Instructors in NLP will often say,

"Do not believe what I'm telling you, just because I say it. Verify everything in your own experience. If it works for you, use it. If not, forget it."

AT BOTH ENDS OF THE SPECTRUM

A person with a strong Internal Frame of Reference will proceed regardless of what anyone thinks. A strong External Frame will think, make decisions and live a life based solely on external feedback. "Oh, my! What will they think?"

In advertising, it is important to appeal to both the internally and the externally oriented person by saying, "You of course will know this is the best product for you by what you say to yourself, or what others will say to you." You may also talk about the purchaser of the product "joining" the group of satisfied owners.

4 AND 5. CONVINCER FILTERS

The Convincer Filter is the filter that someone uses in becoming certain or confident that something is true. The two Convincer Filters tell us how a person becomes convinced (through what Representational System), and how many times a person has to see, hear, do or read something before being convinced.

CONVINCER REPRESENTATIONAL

The first part is the Convincer Representational System. That is, which of the primary representational systems do they use in knowing that someone else does a good job? How do they actually know (visually, auditorially, kinesthetically, or digitally) if a person has done a good job?

QUESTION

"How do you know when someone else is good at what they do? Do you have to..." or **"How do you know that a co-worker is good at their job? Do you have to..."**

A) **See it?** (Then, if you're selling something, you can show it or present pictures.)

B) **Hear about it?** (You can even call these people on the phone, or have them talk to users.)

C) **Do it with them?** (Give them hands-on experience with the product, or give them the product on approval.)

D) **Read about it, or read something they have written?** (Give these people reports, data, letters of recommendation or newspaper articles.)

CONVINCER DEMONSTRATION

The second part of this filter is perhaps more important. The Convincer Demonstration Filter is the time sequence for being convinced—how long it takes someone to become convinced.

QUESTION:

"How often does someone have to demonstrate competency to you before you're convinced?"

A) Automatic

This person assumes a person can do a good job unless that person shows him otherwise. This guy is easy to sell, but watch out because he will buy from the next guy through the door, too. As a manager, this type may be too trusting of an employee's capabilities, and may not check the quality of work often enough. Some managers who are Automatic give the benefit of the doubt to an employee, but then watch very closely to see if the employee makes a mistake.

B) Number of times

This type will have to see it a number of times before he is convinced. They may have to see a number of different products before making a choice. They may have to make a number of visits to the store, or see the salesperson a number of times. To sell them, show the product to them this many times, or let them see several different examples.

C) Period of time

This type wants to have it demonstrated for days, weeks or months before he is convinced. To sell them, give them the product on approval for the specified time.

D) Consistent

This person never gives anyone the benefit of the doubt. He is never convinced. For him, you have to prove it every time. In jobs where quality control is needed, this is the person for the job.

6. MANAGEMENT DIRECTION FILTER

The Management Direction Filter is most suited to business applications, although there are applications to the family unit as well. This filter allows you to determine or predict the suitability of a person for self-management as well as managing others. It will also tell you the ability or desire of a person to manage others and to affiliate with others.

QUESTIONS

There are three questions: **(a) Do you know what you need to do to increase your chances for success on a job? (b) Do you know what someone else needs to do to increase his chances? (c) Do you find it easy or not so easy to tell him?**
Ask all three questions and observe the answers. First determine if he knows what to do for himself, then establish if he knows what others should do, and finally ascertain if he is willing to tell them what to do.

A) Self and Others

(In answering the questions, this person will have answered "yes, yes, yes".) These people are Managers. They know what they need to do, they know what you need to do, and they are willing to tell others.

B) Self Only

(In answering, this person will have answered "yes, no". Third answer does not matter.) These people are NOT managers and they should not be. They do not care what anybody else needs to do, and they really do not care to be managers. They should probably be somewhere in the organization where they are independent.

C) Others Only

(This person will answer no [the boss has to tell me], yes, yes [or no].) These people do well as bureaucrats. They don't know what they need to do, they just do what their supervisor tells them to do. (Often they will have an External Frame of Reference.) They also usually know what you're supposed to be doing, and they sure can tell you!

D) Self but not Others (different strokes for different folks.)

(This person will answer yes, yes, no.) These people usually do not want to be managers. They know what they should do to be a success. They also know what you should do, but are usually unwilling to tell you, saying, "But who am I to tell you what to do?" (If forced to manage, they can sometimes convert to self and others.)

7. ACTION FILTER

This filter has to do with predicting how much energy a person will put into pursuing his life's goals. In addition, it will predict how quickly a person will act.

QUESTION

"When you come into a situation, do you usually act quickly after sizing it up or do you do a detailed study of all the consequences and then act?"

A) Active

They are fairly active—the doers of the world. They will do, and make things happen. An Active person will get things done, a Reflective person will not act until forced to react. They are the people who shape the world—entrepreneurs and go-getters. They go out and do it, they make things happen. They create, they take initiative and they act. They are more likely to make mistakes, but they are also more likely to do *something*.

B) Reflective

Rather than being active, these people tend to study more than act. They let things take their course instead of making things happen. They study the world—i.e., scholars in their ivory towers. A passive type of person, he often will sit back and study things because he is not ready to jump right in until he has had a chance to analyze them. Often they will not act until forced.

They will often do detailed studies, evaluate the consequences fully and then react when forced. They will act IF forced. They say, "Don't do anything rash!" Often bureaucracies get caught in a reactive mode—avoiding mistakes. With this filter, things just seem to happen. "Events in my life are the effect of the events in the world. Rather than being the effect, I am affected by the events."

C) Both

Some people exhibit both traits. They will have the energy to pursue their goals, and will also check to see the consequences, depending on the circumstances.

D) Inactive

They neither study nor act. They ignore events. This person is rare in business and is probably sitting at home.

If additional distinctions are desired, we suggest that a further refinement of these categories could include the following: Super Active, Active, Inactive (Satisfied or Apathetic), Passive, Reflective.

8. AFFILIATION FILTER

The Affiliation Filter deals with how to assign people to a job or to a group effort. It will tell you about the nature of a person's need for affiliation or need for group interaction, and how to assign him in the company.

QUESTION:

"Tell me about a work situation (or environment) in which you were the happiest, a one-time event."

A) Independent Player

They work best by themselves and when in control of their project. They often do not take directions well. (A good person to send off somewhere when you need someone who can be alone to do a job; but they can be unsatisfactory as part of a team.)

B) Team Player

They want to be part of a team and are willing to have their rewards come from a team. They are willing for everything they do to be incorporated into the team. They will be good team players, but may not do well when they are on assignments alone.

C) Management Player

They want to be part of a team, but they also want an area of responsibility all their own. They understand working in a corporate hierarchy. Where possible, they will seek leadership, but will take orders from superiors.

In addition, when you ask this question, you should also note if the answer to the question includes the following information on the Work Preference Filter that follows:

9. THE WORK PREFERENCE FILTER

The Work Preference Filter is important in job assignment, since it indicates a person's preference in working with things, systems or people.

A) **Things:** They prefer to work with things, not people. Mechanics, typists, computer operators, bookkeepers.

B) **Systems:** They will work with people *or* things, but are mostly interested in *how* things or people work. They approach work from the point of view of systems. Computer programmers, linguists, management systems experts, consultants.

C) **People:** They would prefer to work with people. Receptionists, salespeople, managers, personnel directors.

10. PRIMARY INTEREST FILTER

Important in job assignment, the primary interest filter pertains to your primary interest in a given event. We find that a person will be primarily interested in people, places, things, activities or information. For example, your favorite restaurant is your favorite because of your primary interest filter. Some people want to know about who is there, i.e., who else is there? Some people want to know where the restaurant is. Others will want to know what items are on the menu or about the decor. Still others will want to know the speed of the service or what other activities are happening simultaneously. Some will want to know about the history of the restaurant or the recipes for the menu items.

Since the MPVI analysis is context-related, the primary interest can change depending on the context. We often have at least two active at any given time. One of them will be primary. (An additional way to gain rapport is to determine someone's primary filter and match it.)

QUESTION:

The primary interest questions are (use the same question that we used in #8, and/or):
"Tell me about your favorite restaurant." "Tell me about one of your favorite working experiences." "Tell me about one of the top 10 experiences in your life." As the person answers, notice primary interest. Is it in:

A) People: (Who)

Who they are with is important. (This person is interested in people, and will do well when assigned to jobs that deal with people—reception, sales or personnel.) On the job, they may spend a lot of time on the phone or hanging out with others in the office.

B) Place: (Where)

The location, where they are, is important. The location may depend on distance, near or far, or some factor such as convenience. (This person is best assigned according to the location of the office. If the office changes location he may be forced to seek employment elsewhere.)

C) Things: (What)

They are interested in what: possessions, food, money, ambience. (If primary interest is things, and if there is no interest in people in either level of Primary Filter or in the Work Preference Filter, they will be best assigned to computers, typewriters, office equipment, mechanics or machinery.) This person looks for the "right" notebook or the "right" pen. When the going gets tough, the tough go shopping.

D) Activity: (How)

This type is interested in how—what is going on and what they are involved in. Speed of service or what there is to do is important. You might also want to know if internal or external activity is the most important. (In managing this person, make sure that he has a job in which there is plenty to do—one that is not boring.)

We have included time in the activity filter (although perhaps it should be in its own category). Time freaks carry schedulers, calendars or Daytimers. Life centers around the clock. (See the "Time Filters" chapter and "Time Line" section.)

E) Information: (Why, What Information)

This person is interested in "why" or what information is available. They want to know how to do it. They might say, "I just thought you ought to know this." (Give them plenty of information.) It's also important to know if the information they seek is about people, places, things or activities. People who seek information about people are gossips. Information about activity is "how to."

Sometimes there are other categories included in the primary filter. They include sex, money and food. Although they may also be useful, we do not include them in a business context.

SECONDARY FILTERS

In addition, there are secondary filters under the primary classifications. They are:

People: Parents, spouse, friends, boss, associates, employees, strangers.
Things: Toys, clothes, jewelry, electronics, pens, "new stuff."
Activity: Work, home, play, (and what type)?
Information: Ideas, data.

11. CHUNK SIZE FILTER

This filter is very important in communication and in training. It relates to how people best receive and incorporate information. People will prefer either specific (small size, details) information, or global (big picture) information. Most people will move from one to the other, so we also discover which they need to have FIRST. One important use of this filter is the ability to recognize where you are (in terms of chunk size) and the ability to move from big picture to details and back again. This will give you the ability to communicate with anyone. (Also see the "Hierarchy of Ideas" chapter, "Values" section.)

The ability to move from the specific to the abstract has also been associated with intuition, which may just be the ability to chunk up to a larger level of abstraction, discover the relationships and then chunk back down, bringing meaning to certain relationships. This filter is closely related to, although not the same as, the Internal Process Filter, in the Sensor/Intuitor Categories.

QUESTION:

"If we were going to do a project together, would you want to know the big picture first (how it affects the company, nation, etc.), or would you want to get the details of what we're going to do first? Would you really need to know the big picture/details?"

(Ask the opposite of what they selected first.) (In addition, one can observe, based on reading the chapter on the Hierarchy of Ideas, the level of abstraction that a person uses in language or in his interest.)

Asking which they need to have FIRST allows you to know how to give them information in the proper sequence. Some people cannot discover the big picture until they build it from the details. Others cannot get the details until they first have the big picture. The key to successful learning and modeling design is to break the information down into masterable chunks, and then build it up in chunks of a size that makes it impossible to fail.

A) Specific:

They want details. If you chunk too big (are too vague or abstract) for a specific filterer, it will be said that you are giving them fluff, vagueness, irrelevant material. They concentrate on the details of an assignment and may miss the total goal of the project. Details on the sequence of operations may be needed— how to begin and what to do next.

B) Global:

Want you to give them the big picture and little else. They are mostly unconcerned about your giving them the details, or would rather fill in the details themselves. If you chunk too small for a global person, he will be bored. Sometimes they may even miss necessary details. They concentrate on the overall direction of the assignment. These people are good at understanding the context or the pattern, but they may have trouble perceiving and following through in a step-by-step process. They work best when they can delegate details.

C) Specific to Global:

They tend to build up the big picture from the details. Give them the details first or they may be lost in your vagueness. They concentrate on the details of an assignment and how each individual step contributes to achieving that assignment. The process of building the big picture out of the details is called induction. (These people will often prefer bookkeeping or accounting as a profession.)

D) Global to Specific:

Need to have the big picture before they can put the parts in the proper place. They can concentrate primarily on the general direction of the job and have a natural tendency to understand how the big parts of an assignment fit together. This process is often called deduction. (Helpful in sales.)

As a top-notch communicator, you need to be able to chunk at whatever level another person is using. The "Hierarchy of Ideas" chapter is designed to do just that.

CONTEXT AND AMBIGUITY

There are also two important sub-categories in the Chunk Size Filter. The first relates to how much information about context a person needs before being able to take in the details. The second deals with the ability of the person to tolerate ambiguity. In other words, is there a high level of ability in the individual to tolerate ambiguity, and to work with it?

PRESENTATION OF INFORMATION

In addition, there are three ways that people can present information to you. They can present information that is:
1. Descriptive—what is.
2. Evaluative—what ought to be.
3. Interpretive—what you ought to think.

It is also useful to note the following about information presented:
1. Centrality vs. peripherality.
2. The level of abstraction—Concrete vs. abstract.
3. Types of ambiguity:
   Novel—Uncertain, dubious, not enough, information.
   Complex—Too much information.
   Insoluble—Contradictory information.
4. Ways of classifying—Linear, sequential, cybernetic. (Also see the notes on the "Hierarchy of Ideas" for further discussion of chunking, chunk size and the relationship between chunking and intuition.)

12. RELATIONSHIP FILTER

Also called Matching and Mismatching, this filter is a deletion filter. It is of major importance and is one of the most dominant parts of a person's personality. It is one of the systems that we use in the process of understanding and deciding.

Some people, in order to understand something, will look for the similarities. They will match what you are saying with what they know, or they will match the pieces of data to each other. On the other hand, some people, in order to understand something, will look for the differences first. They will Mismatch the data in the process of understanding it. Finally, there are people who do both. These people will go back and forth, matching and mismatching. This filter is not necessarily a set of five exclusive categories, but is a continuum where a person will slide along a scale of the five categories.

Both Matching and Mismatching are important in a business context. (You may find that accountants and lawyers are often trained to be Mismatchers, and salespeople are often trained to be Matchers.)

QUESTION:

The questions to ask to discover this filter are:

"What is the relationship among these three boxes?" *

(Use the above question and one or more of the following if needed.) **"What is the relationship between what you're doing this year on the job and what you did last year on the job?"** (Make sure that the interviewee has had job continuity between the two periods, or change the time periods.) **"When you walk into a room, what do you notice first? (Do you often see a picture at an angle?)"** **"What is the relationship between what you were doing a month ago and what you're doing now?"** **"When you go into a new situation, do you generally notice the similarities or differences first?"** **"What is the relationship between how you feel today and how you felt yesterday?"** To check your postulation ask, **"On the average, how long have you stayed on a job?"**

A) Sameness:

Some people see only sameness. They often say, "It all boils down to this..." When they come into a new situation, they try to

---

*See diagram, next page.

determine whether it is the same as their previous experiences. These people delete massive amounts of information (everything that's different).

Sameness people make up 10% of the United States population. They will stay on a job from 15 years to life, because, "There is no reason to change what I am doing." In an organization, they say, "We need to do things the way we have always done them. There is no reason to change."

Sameness boss to differences employees: "Why do you have to change things all the time? When you have a way that works, why change it?" They want the world to remain the same; they are often conservative. In a relationship, they want things to work all the time. In business, they want sameness and will perhaps be very adamant and mismatch anything that threatens to change their world.

They will want regularity in their work. They will not adapt well to change and may be upset by excessive alteration of what they perceive as their regular work style. In their desire to maintain stability, they may stay with a job for many years. If too much change occurs, they may be compelled to seek employment elsewhere.

Rapport (as taught in NLP trainings) is an exercise in sameness—behaviorally matching and thinking the same as someone else.

B) Sameness with exception:

They see sameness (the largest whole) first, and then differences. They look for what's the same and then point out the exceptions to it. This group comprises 50% of the population and will frequently change jobs every five to seven years. (The Sameness with Exceptions person will often use words like "more"—comparisons about how it was—since "more" is the exception to how it was.) They will initiate or need moderate amounts of change and innovation in their work to fulfill their need for diversity. Salespeople probably need to be Matchers (sameness or sameness with exception).

C) Sameness and Differences Equally:

These people will see sameness and differences equally in coming to understand something. They will seek change and diversity while also valuing stability. They will tend to change jobs every three to five years, and they make up roughly 10% of the population.

D) Differences with exception:

These people see differences before they see how things are the same. In certain circumstances, they will search for the differences and then the similarities. Comprising almost 25% of the population, they will stay in a job 18 months to three years. They often answer, "I'm doing *this* now, I was doing *that* last year, but basically they are the same." (If you have a differences person or differences-with-exceptions person for whom you want to extend job longevity, you will want to create some differences for them at regular intervals on their job.) This type will require variety and difference in their work, and may be intolerant of routine.

In answering the question, some people may say, "Two are the same and one is different." If you get that answer, you need to check further, since they can be either Differences with Exception, Sameness and Differences Equally, or Sameness with Exception.

E) Differences:

They see only differences... "They are all different." They may have trouble seeing patterns or any similarity. The differences people go into a room or a new place and can tell immediately what is wrong, what is not congruent or what is out of place. They comprise roughly 5% of the population. As with the total sameness person, the differences person will delete massive amounts of information. Eighteen months or less is the average length of time they'll stay on a job. Differences people are the ones who want to reorganize an organization—change for change's sake. They are compelled to do things differently all the time, because they want variety.

Imagine a Differences Boss and a Sameness employee. The Boss says, "Why do you always have to do it the same? Why can't you show some creativity?" Successful auditors, proofreaders, lawyers and accountants are often trained to be Mismatch. If this is not their normal preference, they may begin to feel uncomfortable in the career after a number of years.

Motivation:

Someone who is Differences first will be saying, "Not this, not this, not this." In order to motivate someone who is a strong Differences person, give him information to Mismatch. You can say, "I don't know if you'll do this or not." Saying "I don't know" causes them to say, "I do." Saying "If you'll do this" causes them to say "I won't." Then saying "or not" causes their circuits to fry. Embedding the desired motivational command at this point will cause it to go in directly, with little resistance. To a differences person, it is a matter of additional distinctions. Exceptions people view exceptions as a matter of degree, a qualitative difference.

To motivate a Differences with Exception or a Sameness with Exception person to extend his average length of stay, inject some sameness or some differences at that time. A straight differences person will need much change. A business consultant in the Southwest using this Meta Program reduced the turnover in one of his clients simply by hiring based on sameness.

To help a total Matcher (Sameness) or Mismatcher (Differences) develop more balance, have him spend a whole day or week seeing the opposite. (Dissociating them is another way to help them see the exceptions, since both Sameness and Differences people tend to be Associated.)

Additionally, you may want to know what it is that is Matched or Mismatched. Is it ideas, guidance, counter-example (exception to the rule), meta commenting (the little voice that tells us that it will not work), or is it behavior (the polarity response)? Mismatching behavior is a polarity response. To motivate this person, just ask him to do the opposite.

Both Matching and Mismatching are important in a business environment. As we expand knowledge, in a theoretical sense, we:

1. Experience noise
2. Look for patterns in the noise [Matching]
3. Form correlations
4. Express laws

5. Find exceptions to the laws [Mismatching]
6. Find patterns to the exceptions [Matching]

13. EMOTIONAL STRESS RESPONSE

This Meta Program can predict how people will respond in high stress situations. The question is, **"Tell me about a work situation (a one-time event) that gave you trouble."** The purpose of this question is to access a mildly stressful memory. Watch their eye accessing cues, and listen to their predicates. Watch to see if they access kinesthetically as they respond. The categories are:

A) Dissociated

The kinesthetic response is missing in a person who is totally Dissociated—he will not access Kinesthetic at all in answering the question. A Dissociated person may seem to be cold and unfeeling. They react to on-the-job pressure unemotionally, and seem to be unaffected by the emotions of co-workers. They often react unemotionally even when feelings are appropriate. They are good in high-stress situations.

B) Associated

The Associated person will access Kinesthetic, and will stay in the feeling. Usually you will see a change in skin color as they describe the event to you. An Associated person may seem to be too emotional. He is perhaps too associated with his problems. This person is good in a low-stress, personal contact job such as receptionist, flight attendant or therapist. As a manager, the employees will have a feeling that the Associated person cares about them.

C) Choice

A Choice person will access Kinesthetic as he begins to describe the event, and then will come back out of the feelings. While he can respond to a stressful situation in an emotional way, depending on the context, they may then choose to react with thinking or feeling.

14. TIME FILTER

Time has these characteristics—direction, duration, orientation and continuity—how we store our memories, how we access them, how we are oriented to them and how we perceive the continuity of time. Our feeling at this time is that three levels of time filters are important and may deserve further exploration:

TIME ORIENTATION FILTER

The first characteristic that time has is: what is your orientation? Do you have your attention on the past, present or future? Or are you not concerned with time (atemporal)?

A) Past

Includes conservatives, most therapy patients and artists. Carl Jung's category of Feeler is usually someone who is associated to the past.

B) Present

Athletes and doers. Jung called them Sensors (they use their senses in present time).

C) Future

Philosophers, the people who develop new ideas, new developments. Jung's Intuitors are most interested in the future.

D) Atemporal

These people are the people of science. They live outside of time. Jung's Thinkers are usually believed to be Atemporal.

TIME STORAGE (OR PLAYBACK) FILTER

This level deals with how you store your memories in relationship to time. It's interesting, when you stop and consider that you have a way that you store your memories, a way that your brain knows the difference between the past, present and future.

QUESTION:

"I'd like you to STOP... and relax for a moment... and recall a memory from the past... and now an event from the future. Now point to the direction that is the future and the direction that is the past."

The answers will be one of two typical responses:

A) Through Time

"Left to right," or "up to down." (If past, present and future are in front of the plane of the eyes.)

Through Time people have their memories stored left to right. Time is continuous and it may be "long" for them. They are aware of duration. Their memories are usually dissociated. Their memory is what we call temporally sequential—time for them is linear, it has length, it seems long.

They think that time equals value and frequently want to get their "money's worth" in terms of your time. If you spend an hour and a half, they'll want two. For them time and value are often equivalent. "I paid my money and I deserve to get every minute that's coming to me. I want to get all the time I paid for..."

If you have an appointment with them at 2:00 p.m., they expect you to be there at 2:00 p.m., not 2:01 p.m. They often have a hard time "putting their past behind them."

They have collapsed several experiences into a single gestalt and may have difficulty in remembering a specific time; for example, when you ask them to recall a specific time when they were happy, they may have trouble because they have collapsed all happy times into a single experience. So when they access memory, they will be jumping back and forth between a series of experiences. Because of this, their memories are sometimes more dissociated, and it may be harder to anchor a specific experience. If this is the case, you can say to them, "What I'd like you to do now is take pages of your memory and turn them backwards like pages of a book until you find that specific time (snap fingers) NOW..."

B) In Time

"Front to back," or "up to down," or any combination where the past, present or the future is inside or behind the plane of the eyes.

In Time people store their pasts behind them and their futures in front of them. They can go back to one specific point in time, and they can be fully associated at that point. They can go right back to a certain point in time. They are "just where they are," in the now.

Since they are not as aware of duration as the Through Time person, they can be caught up in the now, and may have trouble ending a session. If you have an appointment at 2:00 p.m., they may show up at 2:15 or 2:30 p.m. and think nothing of it. In Time people can be undependable, because they may change their minds more often since decisions are perceived as limiting.

They may frequently need someone to keep them on track, since they can have poor concentration over time, such as in a long term project. They can, however, go into the past and stay there more easily, but often have trouble sorting out tasks. In Time people can go back to a specific time easily. They can, therefore, be anchored in a fully associated state more easily. In time people can be more vivacious but also more easily depressed, because of their total association into the now. They often spend more time in a meeting or talking to someone because they forgot what time it was. When they fail to keep an agreement they may say, "That wasn't me," or "I wasn't myself." In therapy they may have a different problem every week.

TIME ACCESS FILTER

This filter deals with *how* you go back and access your memories.

A) Random Access

These people can RANDOMLY access their memories so that they can jump from now directly to another time, and they can jump between these times easily. They can organize their memories by comparing times. Time has no length. They can hold two times simultaneously, and see time as being a plane. They don't think of a year ago as a long time. They can go back easily in time. They are able to take a meta position regarding time. They can also be at two times at once by bouncing back and forth.

Once convinced they stay convinced. They never forget. They do not experience time in a linear, sequential order. For them time has no length.

B) Sequential Access

These people access their memories SEQUENTIALLY, and so to get a specific memory, they have to start now and run through every event consecutively to go back to that time. For them, time can be long. It's "hard" to go back to a particular memory except sequentially. Some change their minds often, and can be forgetful. They chunk life into sequences that are "over time." To assist a person who is In Time and Sequential Access in recalling a specific memory, you'd say, "I'd like you to rewind the movie of your memory." And if he's through time and over time, you would say, "Turn the pages of your memory backward like a book," as previously discussed. In Time-Random Access people can just jump between memories. (To hypnotize a Sequential-Through Time person, do age regression.)

15. MODAL OPERATOR SEQUENCE

Modal Operators are those words in grammar that talk of possibility or necessity. The Modal Operator Sequence is the sequence of Modal Operators that acts as an undeniable motivator to a person. (Also see Reason Filter.)

This is a most valuable motivation filter and is best discovered by observation over time. Here are some examples of Modal Operators.

MODAL OPERATORS

Can, Can't
Will, Won't
It is Possible, It is Impossible
Could, Couldn't
Would, Wouldn't

May, May not

Must, Must not

Should, Shouldn't

Have to (Got to), Don't Have to

Necessary, Not Necessary

Need to, Don't Need to

The Modal Operator Sequence is what a person says to motivate himself. It is the Auditory digital component of the motivation strategy, and is the sequence of words that moves a person to action. Once you have isolated a sequence, you will want to repeat it to the person to see if he will really act on the series of words that you believe is his Modal Operator Sequence.

Often, people use ineffective Modal Operators. For example, when you hear the words "I should," or "I'll try," you may also realize that you are not hearing a Modal Operator that will produce results.

One way to elicit this filter is to ask, "How did you get up this morning? What was the last thing you said to yourself just before you got up?" Once you have a theory about the words that make up the Modal Operator Sequence for a certain person, keep testing until you discover that they produce results. Check to be sure that you have the right Modal Operator by observing over time.

Another element that you may want to consider is, do THEY produce the Modal Operator, or does it have to come from outside (see Frame of Reference Filter)? One warning, though: a Modal Operator Sequence elicited from memory may be incorrect. So even if you have elicited a sequence you will need to calibrate to see if it produces results.

16. ATTENTION DIRECTION

The Attention Direction is one of the most subtle Meta Programs, and perhaps the most important, especially for communicators, therapists and managers. It deals with how you show other people that you are concerned about their response to you—how you pay attention to them. It is about how other people perceive your paying of attention to them. Do you filter by self or others?

The Attention Direction filter is not directly about self-interest or frame of reference. It is about how you show others your level of interest in them. It, therefore, indirectly deals with attitude. There is no question to ask since this filter is elicited solely by observation. In observing a person's behavior, be sure to calibrate observable behavior and not just the content of the communication. There is a direct correlation between this filter and the External Behavior Filter in the Four Simple Meta Programs.

As you communicate with someone, observe. Do they pay attention to you? Are they *really* paying attention to you? Is their attention outside all the time, or do they go inside? Everyone goes inside for a time to get more information to talk about, but the question is, do they come back out? Does the person you are talking to observe you? Would he notice if you were not there? I have talked to some people and I could have walked away and they would not have noticed! So, the key point is, are they interested in your reaction?

SELF

Someone who filters by self seems to be "inside" most of the time and will seem to be oblivious to other people. A person who filters by self will show it by his posture—sitting back, leaning back. He will have minimal eye contact, and may seem to be oblivious to the outside world in varying degrees. There are also several cultural indicators that one is filtering by self: staring off into space most of the time or talking a mile a minute without looking at the other person.

Someone who filters by self will make assumptions based primarily on his own internal feelings or thoughts. He may discount information that you have to offer. Being internal, they know how well they are communicating by how they feel. They often disregard the reactions of others and rely on their own judgment.

OTHERS

Someone who filters by others will more often seem to be "outside," and will seem to be "paying attention" more than someone who filters by Self.

In the U.S., there are several cultural indicators that show we are filtering by others. They are: posture (leaning toward the other person), eye contact, relationship (being willing to smile, pay attention, responding to non-verbal cues of the other person) and touching people. The person who filters by others is willing to enter other people's models of the world. The best managers, salespeople, therapists and communicators filter by others.

Someone who filters by others will make assumptions primarily based on the other person's reactions. They know how well they are communicating based on information from the outside. They make sense of people's interactions and reactions by paying attention to the results they are producing in the people around them, as opposed to paying attention to how they feel about it. They not only notice other people's reactions but rely on them, believing they are important.

As we mentioned, there is no specific question for the Attention Direction filter. However, one airline that successfully uses this filter for hiring has prospective employees get up and give a talk about themselves to other prospective employees. They then watch to see how the prospective employees in the audience listen to and respond to those prospective employees in front of the room. If the prospective employee fails to pay attention and actively support the person talking by smiling and paying attention to him, then that prospect is not considered for the job. (The airline had determined that 95% of their complaints were about 7% of their employees who filtered by self. By paying attention to this Meta Program in hiring, they went to the lowest complaint record in the airline industry. They feel that it's important for all their employees who deal with the public.)

There are regional characteristics to this filter (of course, this is a generalization). People in the Southwest tend to filter more by others; Easterners, more by self.

OTHER FILTERS

17. GOAL FILTER

The Goal Filter will indicate if a person is a "perfectionist." It will tell you how far people go in attaining their goals. In eliciting this filter, there is no specific question, just look at their goals and see if these people move for:

A) Perfection

Their goals move them toward perfection and they tend to be dissatisfied with their performance.

B) Optimization

Do they do the best with what they've got, which they may use as justification for not doing better.

The Goal Filter is a way of predicting when a person stops. You can ask him to talk with you about a goal he once attained. What was that goal and what did they get? Then what did they do?

18. COMPARISON FILTER

The comparison filter will tell you the nature of comparison that people make as they decide how they're doing.

QUESTION:

"How are you doing on your job? How do you know?"

A) **Quantitative**—Numbers

B) **Qualitative**—Good/Bad

C) **Nature of Comparison**—(Compared to who/what): **Self to Self:** (Past, Present, Future, Ideal). **Self to Others:** (Who?) "He's got more than I do." **Others to Others:** (Who to whom? - gossip)

In sales, determine the nature of the comparison. If it's to an idealized past, then reframe the objection by saying that your product is made the same "old-fashioned way." If it's to an idealized future, then reframe it by saying that your product is always getting better and better.

19. KNOWLEDGE FILTER

QUESTION:

"When you decide you can do something, from where do you get that knowledge?" (Also, knowledge that something is so.)

A) **Modeling/Concepts**
B) **Demonstration**
C) **Experience**—They've done it or seen it done.
D) **Authority**

20. COMPLETION FILTER

This filter tells you if the person has a high or low need for completion. Does he have an aversion to completion? There is a relationship between this filter and the Adaptive Response Filter.

Question:

> "If we were going to do a project together, would you be more interested in the startup phase, where you were generating the energy for the BEGINNING of the project, or in the MIDDLE of the project, where you were involved in the maintenance of the project, or in the END, where you were involved in shutting it down?" and, "Is there a part of the project you'd rather not be involved in?"
>
> People are often better at one part of a project or another, and weak in one part. Using relationships as an example, some people do not like to end a relationship, do not like to say good-bye. These same people are often good at beginning a relationship, and enjoy the chase. In business it is often the same. Take, for example, the salesperson who is excellent at maintaining the account but will not go out and get new accounts; or the converse, the salesperson who is good at getting new accounts but terrible at service.

21. CLOSURE FILTER

This filter is related to how much closure a person needs in dealing with others, or in dealing with information. (This filter is directly related to The Adaptive Response.)

QUESTION

> "Once you have started receiving information that has, for example, four steps, how important is it to you that you receive all four pieces?"

This is an important question in relationship to communication, since the mind tends to forget the content or details of communication when it attains closure. In other words, what you're saying will be more memorable when there are some open loops. (In fact, this is the way that some successful communicators, including Richard Bandler, create response potential in audiences.) Note as you're dealing with a person how much closure they need, and are they able to effectively deal with open loops?

INTERESTING COMBINATIONS

The following combinations of Complex Meta Programs are quite interesting because they can produce rather exotic responses in your client:

Toward, Internal Frame, Active, Possibility, Activity:

In terms of motivation, you might think if I really wanted a good salesperson, I would hire someone who moved toward, had an internal frame of reference, active, a possibility person and who had a high need for activity. (Which, by the way, is the profile of a typical entrepreneur.) This combination will produce a highly active go-getter, but he will be hard to manage unless he agrees with you and is already aligned with you. A balanced frame would help. This person will make a good commission salesperson if he calibrates (sort by others). These types will not look at their sales figures as an indicator of performance because they already know, since they have an Internal Frame of Reference.

Sameness, In Time, Moves Toward: This person massively deletes counterfactual information he doesn't want to hear/see/ etc. If he makes an agreement, he may delete information about it and then say, "I wasn't myself."

Or how about **Differences, Consistent...** "I don't care what you did yesterday, that doesn't matter, what did you do for the company today?" or, "Prove you love me. Every time... differently!!"

15

Changing Meta Programs

How do you change Meta Programs? In general, changing Meta Programs is simple. When you think of Meta Programs consider that they are the strategies that people use in filtering the information that comes to them through the five senses. In addition, Meta Programs are composed of Visual, Auditory, and Kinesthetic representations that are subject to the same submodality manipulations that we use in everyday NLP change work. Additionally, each Meta Program is susceptible to being changed in deep trance or using Time Line Therapy. Having changed Meta Program preferences in almost every category, here are some notes on the process of changing some of the more important Meta Programs that may be helpful:

BASIC META PROGRAMS

EXTERNAL BEHAVIOR

Introvert and Extravert are a result of decisions that a person has made in the past regarding how he will react with other people. A significant emotional experience will usually be the determining factor as to whether a person is an Introvert or an Extravert. To change the person from one to the other, just identify the significant emotional experience using Time Line and disconnect the decision to be a certain way.

INTERNAL PROCESS

Internal Process is related to a person's ability to chunk and his preference in chunking. Just have them read the chapter on the "Hierarchy of Ideas", and give them chunking exercises.

INTERNAL STATE

Internal State is directly related to the person's being Associated or Dissociated. Anchoring is most useful in this process.

THE ADAPTIVE RESPONSE

Since there is a high degree of correlation between Judger and Through Time, and between Perceiver and In Time, to switch a person from one to the other, just change his Time Line, from front to back to right to left, or vice versa.

COMPLEX META PROGRAMS

DIRECTION FILTER

The Direction Filter is made up of a series of values (and in some cases general beliefs) that we move Toward or Away From. First find out what the elements that the person is moving toward or away from are. The Direction Filter is a major part of a person's personality. The values that are a part of this filter are a result of the experiences that a person has in his life.

One of the theories that we've been working on recently regarding this filter is that every Toward value, where coupled with a statement like, "Oh, I don't need that," indicates the opposite Away From value as an "unhealed" need underlying the Toward value. You might say, for example, "Bill, what do you want in a relationship?" Bill says, "Oh, I don't need a relationship. I'm too busy." We might then conclude that Bill had an unhealed Away From value regarding a relationship. There is another theory, closely aligned to this theory, that every Toward value is the result of a significant emotional experience, of an Away From nature which is of a negative nature.

EXAMPLE

Tad: "What's important to you about being in business?"

Fred: "Freedom."

Tad: "Why freedom? Freedom for what purpose?"

Fred: "To express who I am. To be creative."

Tad: "Why do you need to express who you are? What's important to you about that?"

Fred: "It feels good and I also don't want to be stifled."

Tad: "What experiences have you had of being stifled in the past?"

Fred: "I flashed on my Dad."

So we have a very high value of Freedom, which indicates its opposite value of not being stifled, because he flashed on some unhealed stuff about his dad.

Our point of view at this time is that many of the values in our hierarchy of values have behind them unhealed values that are the opposite. One of the problems that a person who simultaneously moves both Toward and Away From (regarding the same value) has is that the mind cannot hold a negation. For example, don't think of a blue tree. What are you thinking of? Of course, a blue tree. So if, like Fred, I am moving Toward freedom, and simultaneously Away From being stifled, I am holding "not being stifled" in my mind as an internal representation.

We already know that the internal representation in my mind is going to determine my state, and therefore my results. So holding "not being stifled" in my mind is going to create a result of being stifled. In fact, we notice that people who move Toward and Away From simultaneously are not only incongruent, but also create little events in their past that are exactly what they have been avoiding.

If we heal the opposite, Away From value (using Time Line Therapy), then the Toward value will move down in the hierarchy. It may even disappear from the hierarchy. While you will have cleaned up the incongruency, and stopped the little disasters, you will have lessened the driving force behind the Toward value. So, depending on your outcome, you may need to move the Toward value back up in the hierarchy using submodalities. (See "Values" page 201.) When an Away From value is healed, and the conflict is in many cases ended, the person will have more desire to pursue values of a higher purpose.

When you integrate values conflicts that exist among parts, using the Visual Squash, (see page 189) the value(s) involved will move upward in the hierarchy.

If you heal a very strong, totally Away From value, you probably should replace it with a Toward value of some kind, because they should have something to move Toward.

To heal an unhealed Away From value that is in conflict with a Toward value, using Time Line Therapy, say, "I could guess which memory we're talking about, about which one it really is, but there was a certain event in your past that caused you to have this need. The one root cause. There was a time back then that you made a certain decision about how life was regarding this value. Do you remember? Good. Go back to that time. Good. And notice what emotions were present in your body at the time you made the decision. What are the emotions? (They name the emotions.) Now float above your Time Line, and go back 15 minutes before it all began. Good. Now, let me ask you a question. Now, where are the emotions? And the decision. Has it disappeared too?" (For additional information on this process see page 9.)

Another way to heal past traumas is to say, "Do you see the younger you in that memory? Good. She's upset, isn't she? Yes, she is. Can you float down into that memory, and tell the younger you that you're from the future, and that you survived? Give her a big hug. She's happier now, isn't she? Now, ask her if she wants to come out of there and come with you. She wants to, doesn't she? What I'd like you to do is to float with the younger you to a grassy field or meadow, and just lie there on your back and watch the clouds go by, and notice how good it feels to be away from all that. I want you to tell her that she'll never ever have to go back there again. That she's done with that time, and she'll never ever have to go back again. Does she want to stay with you? Good. Is it OK if she stays with you? Good. Bring her inside and make a special place for her."

A third way, after they're in the memory, is to ask, "And what did you need in that experience from the other person there in order to feel totally whole, totally positive about yourself?" They say, "Love and respect." You say, "Good. I'd like you to imagine a source of infinite love and respect flowing from a source above your head, flowing through you, and out your heart to them. And what is the expression on his face when it hits him? Good. Just let it continue until the entire situation is healed."

Then, as you have the person float back up above his Time Line and come forward to the present, suggest to him that "The things that you decided in the past are just that. In the past. And you now have new choices and new possibilities about your relationship to (the value). And I'd like you to notice as you come to the present that your choices increase geometrically until you come to now, and notice that it's all OK."

These tend to leave the entire situation "healed," and will dramatically affect or even delete the Away From value that is underlying the Toward value, and can even change an Away From person to a Toward person.

FRAME OF REFERENCE

I have had excellent results with changing people using deep trance to change them from External Frame of Reference to Internal Frame of Reference. Just have them walk down a flight of 70 steps, and notice that they are at the deepest level. Then tell them that they are going back up to 65 which everybody knows is the level of the Meta Programs. Then suggest that they look off to the right, where they will see the switch that comprises the Frame of Reference Filter. Tell them to notice that it is flipped to, say, External. Now have them flip it to Internal. Finally, have them come back up the steps to the top.

CONVINCER

The source of the Convincer Demonstration filter will be the experiences that the person has had and the decisions they have made. This type of construction is best changed using Time Line.

RELATIONSHIP

The Relationship Filter is based on the interaction of three of the Simple Filters. They are: Internal Process, Internal State and

Adaptive Response. A person who is total Sameness *or* total Differences is probably quite Associated in making the comparison. In fact, try this: Make an associated picture and then try and bring up another picture for comparison. Impossible for most people! Shifting a person from Sameness to Sameness with Exception, or from Differences to Differences with Exception, is a matter of getting the person to Dissociate. Anchoring is helpful.

ATTENTION DIRECTION

The source of the Attention Direction filter will also be the sum total of the experiences that the person has had, the training (or social training) and the decisions they have made regarding paying attention to other people. This type of construction is best changed using Time Line.

IV

Values

16

Introduction To Values

INTRODUCTION

Throughout the ages, values have been the justification for prejudice and strife and have often been the cause of simple lack of communication. More than any other element in therapy, values are at the root of change and have a major effect on the longevity of the changes we make.

VALUES DEFINED

So, what are values? They are what we move toward or away from (see Meta Programs). Values are usually expressed as nominalizations. (A nominalization is a process word, like "communicating," turned into a noun, "communication.") Values are those things (or notions) that we are willing to expend resources for, or to obtain resources to have. Values are largely unconscious, and at the deepest level they drive a person's true purpose as a human being. Values govern ALL human behavior. First, they provide the push or the kinesthetic drive as prior motivation for our actions. Second, they serve as after the fact evaluation criteria, or judgment about our actions. Values are the way we judge good and bad, right and wrong, appropriateness and inappropriateness.

So that we are talking the same language, let us agree on some additional definitions:

HIGHLY VALUED CRITERIA

Highly Valued Criteria are also values. They are our major, most important values around which we organize beliefs. They are also expressed by nominalizations such as satisfaction, security, enjoyment, challenge, accomplishment and honesty.

You might think of a value or highly valued criterion as being like a cup hook. You know, a cup hook—the kind that hangs in a cabinet, holding cups. Can you imagine how that looks? Imagine that a highly valued criterion or value is like a cup hook. Hanging from it, just like cups hanging on cup hooks, are a number of beliefs.

BELIEFS

Beliefs are hooked, or related, to values. Every individual belief you have is "hooked" or linked to a certain value that is probably unconscious. Beliefs are more conscious than values, and are generalizations about our actions, about what we are doing or about what we need to do. They are statements about our internal representations—about how we believe the world is.

BELIEF SYSTEMS

A belief system is a cluster of beliefs arranged around a highly valued criterion. Imagine a tree where each major limb holds a value, and around each value are a number of smaller branches that are beliefs. The entire system of branches or beliefs we will call a belief system. Beliefs are generalizations about our actions and about what we are doing and about what we need to do.

CORE BELIEFS AND VALUES

Core beliefs and values have to do with our identity and are often created unconsciously in as simple a way as watching our parents interact before we were age 8. These core beliefs and values are the most pervasive. The ones that impact us the most are the ones that are outside our awareness. Core beliefs and values are the most unconscious of the values and probably the most important in terms of defining our personality. So core values are going to be the kinds of values that serve as the basis for our personality. Core beliefs and values are like Highly

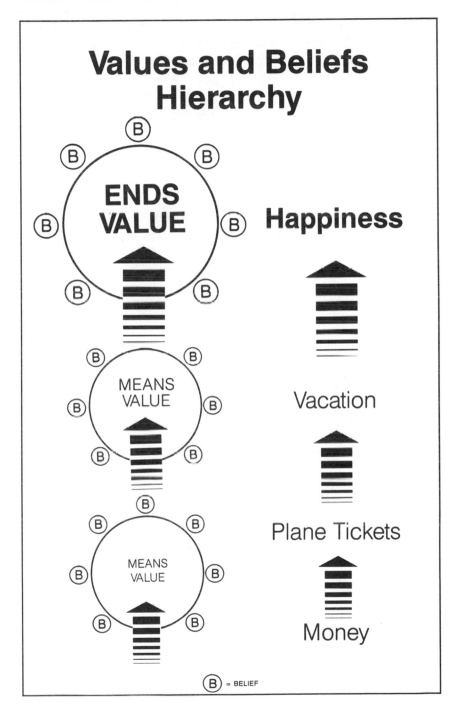

Values and Beliefs Hierarchy

Valued Criteria, but what differentiates them is that the core beliefs and values are the most unconscious parts of our identity.

In addition, when dealing with the psychology of health, it is important to recognize that people have beliefs and values around cause and effect, meaning (or complex equivalence), boundaries and capabilities, and that these effectively control our actions (especially regarding our health or lack of it).

HIERARCHIES

In our minds, we unconsciously arrange our values in hierarchies. As we evaluate our actions, the more important values are usually searched for first. After the more important values are found and satisfied, then the next most important ones become important.

INCONGRUITIES

Incongruities are usually the result of values conflicts in a person. A person who has internal values conflicts will display either simultaneous incongruency (such as by shaking his head "yes" and saying "no"), or sequential incongruency (such as "I want to do this, but..."). If values are not aligned with the changes you made in therapy, then typically the changes will regress. The Visual Squash reframe and other reframing processes are excellent for handling values and beliefs conflicts.

UNCONSCIOUS MODELING

Our values are often a result of our unconscious modeling of people around us. We adopt belief systems and values in order to fit in. A new hamburger-loving employee, working for a company of vegetarians, may adopt their ways to establish more rapport with the group. Then, as he later ponders his actions, he may actually adopt new values as he remembers eating a vegetarian meal. Beliefs are often created in just this way. We do something and then we say, "I acted that way, so I must believe such and such." In other words, our beliefs and values are often a result of, as well as a justification for, our actions. We also judge our actions based on our consistency. That is, we find ourselves doing something and then justify it by saying that the action represents a belief. The represented belief may indeed be in conflict with a previously held belief, but we change the belief in order to remain consistent. (It might be obvious, therefore, that you might not want to hang around with people you do not want to emulate.)

ATTITUDES

Attitudes are based on belief systems. Attitudes rest on clusters of belief systems relating to a certain subject, so they are formed by clusters of beliefs and values. An attitude, therefore, is the sum total of our beliefs and values on a certain subject.

BEHAVIOR

In modeling behavior and determining how behaviors are formed, we believe that besides internal processing strategies, internal states or emotions and physiology, one should consider two types of values. First, there are values that are sources of power (values like the ability to accomplish) and sources of determination (values like free will). Second, there are values and beliefs about the way the world operates in relationship to other people (values like fairness). These combine to determine our state at the moment that determines behavior.

Many therapeutic processes work only on the level of changing strategies, state or physiology. Changes made at this level unfortunately often tend to be short-lived. If you also change values, beliefs and attitudes in addition to changing strategies, state and physiology, it will result in a more permanent change in behavior. We have discovered that using the Time Line, Visual Squash and changing values produces change that is substantially more generative and more long-lasting. In fact, without taking values and the parts that maintain them into account, the change produced is likely to be more short-term and not lasting. Therefore we recommend making sure that values, beliefs and attitudes, and the parts that support them, are taken into account when determining the type of therapeutic approach.

ARRANGEMENT IN THE MIND

How are all these pieces arranged in the mind? Meta Programs are the most unconscious. Values are the next most conscious, beliefs the next most conscious, attitudes the next most. While we're moderately conscious of our attitudes, we're reasonably unconscious about most of our values.

Totally Conscious

    Attitudes

    Beliefs

    Values

    Core Values

    Meta Programs

Totally Unconscious

In addition, Memories and Decisions may fall anywhere in this chart from conscious to unconscious.

Once a person begins doing values research or begins looking at values, of course, he will become more conscious of his values and they will also become more dissociated from them. For the most part, however, people are unconscious about their values and completely unconscious about their Meta Programs.

17

The Formation of Values

In discussing the formation of values we draw on research done by the sociologist Morris Massey, who says that young people go through a series of developmental periods in the creation of their major core values. There are three major periods that a person will go through in values and personality formation. The three major periods are the **Imprint Period**, which occurs from birth until age 7, the **Modeling Period**, which is from 8 to 13 and the **Socialization Period**, from 14 to 21.

THE IMPRINT PERIOD

The Imprint Period, from birth to age 7, is the time when we are like a sponge. We pick up and store everything that goes on in our environment. We get our basic programming in that **Imprint Period**. Our basic programming occurs between ages 2 and 4, and by the time a child is 4, most of the major programming has occurred.

Using that data, I've been able to help a person overcome a long-term phobia in as little as 10 minutes. Most of the phobias that I have worked with were created between ages 3 and 7. That is where we find most of the earliest experiences that serve as the basis for a phobia. (Of course, there may be amplifications or reinforcement of the phobia after that.) There may also be no remembrance of the creation of the phobia because the learning processes that occur during the Imprint Period are largely unconscious. The Imprint Period occurs from ages 0 to 7 and is the basic programming of an individual. The child unconsciously picks up the parents' behavior.

MODELING PERIOD

The ages 8 through 13, according to Massey, are the Modeling Period. Between 8 and 13 the child begins to consciously and unconsciously model basic behaviors. I can plainly remember a time when I was about 10. I was with my grandfather, who had a rather severe limp. I was unconsciously mimicking his way of walking. He saw me and scolded me for doing that, and yet at the time I was not aware I had been copying him. Perhaps you, too, can recall memories of how you modeled adults during this time. Maybe you can even remember having to dress just like Mommy or Daddy.

Before age 7 or so, the child is mostly unaware of any difference between the parents and himself. The child experiences no difference from parents. Then at age 8 the child begins to notice that there are people outside himself, and through age 13 he begins to look outside himself at the goings on in the world. They notice the behavior of friends and family and model them. At that point, children begin to develop heroes. We notice that children have fewer conscious heroes before age 7 than after; from age 8 to 13 they begin to start picking up the values of the people they have made into heroes. Massey's point of view is that our major values about life are picked up between 8 and 13 (at around age 10). In addition, his point of view is that your values are based on where you were and what was happening in the world when you were 10. More on this later.

SOCIALIZATION PERIOD

Ages 14 through 21 we call the Socialization Period. The child goes through a Socialization Period where social interaction begins with other human beings. The young adult here picks up relationships and social values, most of which will be used throughout the rest of his life. At age 21, values formation is just about complete. At this point core values do not change unless there is a significant emotional experience (or other therapeutic change is done). Using techniques described in this chapter, we can change the values in a matter of several minutes.

Other than through NLP intervention, core values do not change unless there is a significant emotional experience. Other, more conscious values change and evolve continually. People change and grow and their values change over time. The values people start with, however, the basic core values, are formed around age 10 and locked in at age 21.

When you want to do effective values change work, Time Line therapy will be one way to accomplish this. Go back, find and change the memories from the Imprint Period, the Modeling Period and the Socialization Period that were important in the formation of the particular value. You may have noticed that hypnotherapists, when working with memories to make changes in people, will usually work with ages 0 to 21. Similarly, with Time Line Therapy there is often no need to work on memories that are formed after the person is 21. In fact, when doing change work using Time Line, it is always preferable to use a memory before 21. The reason is that in Time Line, we are operating on the most significant event in these particular periods. So in doing values change work, you want to look at these periods and discover what significant experiences occurred then.

THE SOURCES OF VALUES

Now what are the sources of an individual's values that you will find when you go back in the Time Line and look for particular memories? Where did those major values come from? What are the influences that create our core values? They come from our environment. People who grew up at different ages are going to have different values based on significant events that occurred in their environment around age 10.

FAMILY

The first is the family. The child is going to model friends and parents. For example, if you were working on a weight problem, you would probably go back and discover how and when they created the internal model that created the problem. Were their parents fat? Were their friends fat? What is the mental image that they have of their size at age 8, 10 or 13? Did they say, "... gee, I want to be just like that person?" Go back in their Time Line and discover when they decided to be like that person, which usually occurs during the Imprint or the Modeling Period, but may occur as late as the Socialization Period. Next, what characteristics do people in the family have? Are the men real macho and the women passive? Or are the women strong and the men not? You will want to investigate the Imprint Period for experiences that formed certain family values—family is most critical during the Imprint Period.

FRIENDS

Values of friends will have serious impact during the Socialization Period. By the time the child is a teenager, through age 21, friends will have the major impact. Remember that by this time, the children are theoretically on their own and doing extensive modeling of friends.

RELIGION

You will also want to look at church or religion. What exposures did the person have to church or religion during these periods? Which religion and what did that religion teach that has meaning for the presenting problem of the client?

SCHOOL

School and teaching techniques will also determine your values. Did you have choice in school? Did you have no choice in school? Was the school integrated? Were the teachers sexist (telling you that women were no good) or racist (saying that Blacks were no good)? Any of these that occurred during school will affect your values. Textbooks will also affect your values. What did the textbooks say? Did you grow up reading "Fun With Dick and Jane" (which is quite sexist, by the way)? Did the teacher treat you as someone who could learn, or as stupid? We have proven that a teacher's beliefs will have a major effect on the students' grades. Finally, even the physical setup of the classroom will unconsciously affect learning. Everything that occurred in school will have had an effect on a person's values.

GEOGRAPHY/LOCATION

Geography, where you grow up, affects your values. Did you grow up in the South or North (racial values)? Did you grow up in the East or the West (social values)?

ECONOMICS/PROSPERITY

Was the family prosperous? People who were age 10 during the Depression, which was 1930 roughly, are 70 now. This particular group of people say, "I don't want my children to want for anything." That is a major core value for anybody who was age 10 in 1929. "I want to make sure that I provide them with anything they need. I want to make sure they have it better than I did."

Today, statistically, Americans are saving less than ever before. Why? Because that particular value is gone. The people who save are the 70-year-olds who went through the Depression. People who grew up in the 70s never knew that problem because their parents went overboard. They said, "I don't want MY children to want for anything." Consequently, their children do not know what saving is about. They do not have any values around saving and so they are not saving money. Not saving is a result of their values.

MAJOR HISTORICAL EVENTS

People my age were 10 about the time of the war in Korean, and we began to prepare to be attacked. We had air raid drills in school, remember? We all crouched under our desks, as if that would save us from an atomic bomb! Then I saw atomic bombs tested in the Nevada desert on television, and I *knew* that the desks would not save us.

So what are some of the values that were programmed then? Or how about during the Korean war? Attack the people in North Korea! Blow up everybody! From that day forward, we were living with the threat of the A-bomb. So look and see what major events occurred around age 10 for you and your client. Those are going to set your core values and beliefs, which are the major value indicators you have.

THE MEDIA

Let us look at the media for a minute. Media is a major programming piece for values from ages 8 to 21.

How about music? Lyrics in music are programming the values of an entire generation. Listen to and watch the songs children listen to and watch from ages 15 to 21. You will be able to predict what their values will be when they become adults.

Television is now a major force in setting values. That didn't happen in previous generations. Television is now virtually in one hundred percent of homes. Since the 1950s people have had television at home during their entire lives. Most young people today do not remember times without television.

Television has created a belief in "now," so anybody age 10 in 1950, or older, has the belief that they can have (or at least the desire to have) anything they want now. That is the result of the underlying current of television commercials, which is, you have a headache, take this pill and the pain disappears. In 30 seconds we can solve all the world's problems simply. If 30 seconds is not enough, then solve them in a half-hour program.

VALUES DIFFER

Every generation in America today has different values, based on significant experiences that occurred when they were 10 years old. Let us look at some of the major age groups in America today and the significant experiences that happened in their lives when they were 10.

AGE 70s

They were in their early 70s in 1980, so their major programming occurred in 1920. They were 10 in the 1920s. It was just after World War I. We made the world "safe for democracy." There was intense patriotism. Short hair for men became necessary because of the war (long hair didn't fit under a helmet), and hair length was how you knew if a person was patriotic or not! That was how you knew a person was OK. At the same time, the family was very close and the woman's place was in the home.

Contrast this with 1985, when 55% of mothers were working out of the home; statisticians tell us that by 1989 85% will be employed (which means that a woman's place is and will be "out of the home"). But in the early "20s, the men were the bread winners! Then, their jobs were everything. They worked long hard hours in often dangerous conditions. Jobs, and even life were the same. People were total Sameness. (See the Relationship Meta Program.) People expected to grow up, live and die within a few hundred miles of where they were born.

It was a "good" world, then. Many people in this group are now wondering what has happened to the world. They think the world has gone to hell and they cannot understand the younger people.

AGE 60s

They were in their early 60s in 1980, and their major values programming occurred in 1930 after the collapse of the stock market.

Today they are the leaders in society—bank presidents, college presidents, corporate heads—our leaders. Now, what did this do? It made this group quite unsure about the future and very concerned about security. They are interested in financial security (which is evidenced by money).

This age group is motivated by money! Security! Their heroes included Tom Mix, Hopalong Cassidy and Amelia Earhart. Like these heroes, this group is convinced that the good guys always win. Sex and bad language were forbidden.

AGE 50s

People in their early 50s in 1980 had their intense programming in the 1940's when we were at war. Everything turned to the war effort, and thus began the destruction of the American family unit. This is the generation where change began to be programmed into the family unit. "How're you going to keep 'em down on the farm after they've seen Paree?" Before this we were programmed to stay in the same geographic area from birth to death. From this moment on we were programmed to move.

AGE 40s:

People in their 40s in 1980 were programmed in the 1950s by another war, the Korean War. In 1950, the good life had arrived, and General Electric made a major marketing decision. They decided to let consumers have what they wanted—what a surprise to American business! This was a departure from past marketing where, for example, Henry Ford had said, "You can have any car as long as it's black." But G.E.'s thought was very different and a radical departure from the past. People could truly have what they wanted. At the same time the parents from the Depression said, "My kid is going to have it better." So they gave, and because these were boom times, they had more to give. The children took! Concurrently, Dr. Spock was being misinterpreted, and so parents indulged children with permissive programming. (Dr. Spock later said that misinterpreting his books had messed up a whole generation.) The atomic bomb made us a "live-for-now" generation. "Live it up, you're in the Pepsi Generation!!"

Then TV exploded on the scene and it changed all generations to come. Among other things, TV moved our values from "good guys win" to "bad guys win." We saw Charles Van Doren ("$64,000 Question" scandal), and Steve McQueen ("Thomas Crowne Affair") do things and get away with them, things that in previous generations would have caused major scandals.

In the 1950s there was a major shift in values in America and we were never to be the same. The explosion of information since the 1950s ushered in an era of perpetual change—the rate of change increased dramatically. We now have jet planes, television, cable, computers, cellular telephones—instant communication! Now, values shifts may be as close as three to five years apart.

AGE 30s

These people were 10 in 1960 and they are truly the Television Generation. TV is so exciting that nothing in life is exciting anymore! The U.S. space program is an example of these changing values. Do you remember when we reached the moon for the first time? But two years later it was "ho- hum" when the television networks got complaints as they pre-empted the daytime soaps for a moon landing. What else was on television then? Two Kennedys and Martin Luther King's assassinations. The Vietnam War. And don't forget drugs. What values did this instill? First of all, this group tends to be scared, and they think differently.

This age group thinks that television has been around forever, and that computers are normal. They also understand and believe in Ecology.

AGE 20s and TEENS

This group was in its 20s in 1980. For this group who were 10 in 1970 there has been another major shift. There are no great American heroes of the 80s. Our heroes are now the likes of J.R. Ewing! What a hero. Then the ultimate scandal—Watergate, where the President and the Vice President were involved. As if all that was not enough to send a message to the 10 year olds who were watching, President Ford pardoned President Nixon as if to say, "It's OK, do it, just don't get caught." These people understand computers and take them for granted. Some cannot remember what it was like without them. They assume the existence of jet planes and space travel. They find school VERY boring compared with life, and they find life boring compared with TV and MTV!!

THE MAJOR GROUPS

Those are the values groups by decade. Now, what is happening in the world in the 1980s? As we look at the values operative in each group, we can see essentially four major groups that we will call Traditionalists, Harmonizers, Rejectionists and Synthesizers.

TRADITIONALISTS

The Traditionalists are in their 70s, 60s, 50s and mid 40s. They are in control of the system that they built. Being group/

team-oriented, they love to get together and do things like company picnics. They tend to look up to authority figures and believe in the law, the boss, the president. Typically they will accept the leader blindly and do not question his commands.

They believe in social order. A favorite saying is, "Everything in its place and a place for everything." They believe that they are discriminating in their tastes. They are Puritanical; if they have fun, they certainly do not talk about it. They are very formal in dress and demeanor. They believe in work for work's sake. A job is a job, not meant to be fun. For them, stability equals money. Change, any change, is a threat to their economic security. Much of life is devoted to looking for the "right way" to do it (and, "once I find that, my life will be smooth forever"). They are problem-oriented and believe the best way to solve a problem is to form a committee. They are very much into materialism. They love things and collect things. In work, time off without pay is a threat.

HARMONIZERS

They are in their mid-40s to mid-30s. They are like the rejectionists but were programmed by traditionalists. They worry about just missing "it." They are very erratic in the marketplace. They are into self-help books, seminars and (according to the President's Commission Report on Pornography) are the primary purchasers of pornography. Whereas the traditionalist will not buy pornography and the rejectionist does not need it, the harmonizer purchases it because he thinks he just missed the entire sexual revolution.

REJECTIONISTS

They are in their mid-30s to mid-20s and have very different values from the previous groups. They reject traditionalist values. They do not believe in group or team. They are individualists. To them, rules and regulations do not apply. They do not accept authority just because someone is in authority. They need to discuss, question, ask why. They want to participate in decisions that affect them. They believe in social change and push for equality.

They are sensual—they have fun and talk about it. Profane language is normal. They tend to be informal, very informal in their dress and action. Work is not as important as it is to the traditionalist. Their job is a small portion of life and they look to it for meaning, self-fulfillment and fun. Fun is equal to stability. Change is a constant—they get bored so they need change. They are "instant-solution" oriented. At work, they may not be fully accountable and can be cause-oriented. They buy something for the experience of the thing and then they throw it away. Time off without pay is great!!! Overtime is a threat.

SYNTHESIS

They are in their mid 20s to teens, and are very confused and worried about their future. They know the quantity (not necessarily the quality) of American life will have to go down. They realize that the "amount" in their life is going to get less. This realization seems to be producing more conservative behavior.

IMPLICATIONS

These are the major core values systems that are operative in people today in the United States and they indicate major implications for marketing. Knowing by which group your product or service is consumed will allow you to market to their values and increase your ability to sell to them.

In the process of assisting a person to change, you can take into account his values as a basis and as leverage. Values are not fixed in stone and people tend to grow, change and evolve.

We have also found that people tend to change their values from time to time. However, the core values a person has change slowly if at all. In addition, there will also be a certain set of values that changes over time. (This is discussed in the "Evolution of Values".) In the process of changing someone's values you will want to take into account how they were created, what changes have happened to their values, and how the values change.

18

The Evolution of Values

In addition to our basic or core values, there is a whole group of values that grow and evolve over time. According to the late Claire Graves, a professor at the University of the State of New York at Schenectady, people grow and their values evolve and change over time.

In an article published in the *Journal of Humanistic Psychology,* in the Fall 1970 edition (Volume 10, No. 2), Graves said that the "... adult man's psychology, which includes his values, develops from the existential states of man. These states emerge as man solves certain hierarchically ordered existential problems crucial to him in his existence." In other words, adult men and women go through a series of existential values, problems and solutions that determine their attitudes and personality at the time. Interestingly enough, (and I invite you to look at your past for verification of this viewpoint), the problems we experience at one level of existence are not actually solved; they just become inconsequential as new coping mechanisms are begun in the process of change. "The solution of man's current problem of existence releases free energy in his system and creates in turn new existential problems."

A SERIES OF VALUE SYSTEMS

Dr. Graves postulates a chain of value systems that grows and evolves as a human grows and evolves. Graves said that as of 1970, there were seven that were significant. Since then, more value systems have evolved and continue to evolve as time goes on. (We have begun to mention the additional levels in our seminars and trainings.) Here are some characteristics of Graves' seven levels:

LEVEL ONE—SURVIVAL
"Express Self Now for Survival"

At this level survival or subsistence is the major problem of existence that a human is faced with. The first level is man living alone or with his family, grubbing for roots and berries to survive. At this level, man is seeking the immediate satisfaction of his basic physiological needs in a Pavlovian (conditioned) way. When man solves the problem of the struggle to maintain physiological stability in order to exist, he moves to the second level. There are probably no people functioning at the number one level on the earth today.

LEVEL TWO—TRIBAL
"Sacrifice Self Now for the Tribe and the Wishes of the Chief"

Man's need for stability, safety and for continuation of his way of life moves him into the second level, where men band together to form a tribe. This is the first of the sacrificial levels, and the wishes of the individual are subservient to the wishes of the chief. At this level time is seasonal, as opposed to there being months, days or even hours. There is no difference between man and the rest of the world. There are no clear borders between the self and the world.

Existence is based on myth and a mystical tradition full of spirits, magic and superstition. When the tribe's survival is assured and relative safety is assured, the conditions necessary for the creation of the third level have been met. The movement to the third level begins when the barriers to insight are removed and insight (either the ability to have one's own insights or to be able to perceive the significance of the other's insights) occurs. As this happens man begins to perceive that there are others—other men, other animals and even the spirits—that are waiting to fight him. So he sets out in heroic fashion to conquer them all.

LEVEL THREE—RED NECK
"Express self now, the hell with others"

This level often begins with dissonant youth who are not troubled by memories of the past and who are capable of original thought. This way of life is based on the Agricultural Revolution and depends on loyalty and service. Power is its own law, saying: "I am the law in this town." As in the old West, "might is right." Over time these laws are translated into the absolute right of kings, the prerogatives of management and even the right of the hustler to all he can hustle.

This level serves as the psychological basis for the Knights of the Round Table, Rambo and even Bonnie and Clyde. But the expressiveness of this system brings the seeds of its end. The third level of existence does not answer the question of "why." Why are there "haves" and "have-nots?" As man enters into the next stage his success or lack of it causes him to become convinced that the conditions of "have" and "have-not" are part of a directed design. Death still faces him and he discovers a need to reconcile the question of an afterlife.

LEVEL FOUR—THE SYSTEM
"Sacrifice Self Now for Salvation (or Attainment) Later"

This level of existence can be, in some expressions, saintly. The question of existence has been temporarily resolved by sacrifice. Man has discovered that this world is not for ultimate pleasure. This is based on the perception of unending struggle in a threatening universe that existed in Level 3. Here man decides that there are certain rules that are prescribed for each class of men, and the rules describe the way that each class should behave (the basis for the caste system in India). The rules are the price man has to pay for his more lasting life.

This level describes the likes of the Communist Party, the Catholic Church and the U.S. Federal Government. This is the level where most American government workers and many heads of major corporations are. Historically, in the American West, the emergence of this system came after the gunfighter (Level 3), and it was expressed as, "We need a government of laws, not men."

After a time, when security is achieved through this system, some of the members begin to question the cost. Some of the people begin to ask why they cannot have some pleasure in this lifetime. The result is that man sets out to build a new life for pleasure here and now.

LEVEL FIVE—ENTREPRENEUR, MATERIALIST
"Express Self Now, but Calculatedly for Material Rewards Now"

Man now seeks to conquer the world by learning its secrets, rather than through sheer force and power. This is the entrepreneurial spirit that built the Industrial Revolution and the American business spirit. This is Lee Iacocca at his best. Level Five man develops the scientific method and is assured that science will solve all the world's problems. But this level is not without its problems. Man achieves the good life, but the price is again too high. He finds he is not liked by others who resent his use of knowledge for himself. He is envied and respected but not liked. He has achieved status but is rejected (even by his own children), and so he begins the move to the next level.

LEVEL SIX—THE MOVEMENT
"Sacrifice Self Now, for Self Actualization for Self and Others"

People at this level of existence become concerned with belonging, being accepted by others, not being rejected and with knowing the inner self. Social acceptance is more important than "progress." Level Five man has raped the earth and other men to achieve his progress. Level Six rejects these values. Consensus management is the only way to manage. Human harmony is the most important value. When the harmony of the group and self-realization for self and others is achieved, man is restless to move on.

Level Six also brings with it a series of problems. Level Six organizations tend to bog down in group consensus and not achieve results. In addition, there is more emphasis on feeling good than on producing, and so some sixes notice that there are people taking advantage of the system and that the system supports people who should, perhaps, not be supported. It is here that man begins to cross to a whole new dimension of understanding.

LEVEL SEVEN—EXISTENTIAL
"Express Self Now, but not at the Expense of Others or the World, so that Life May Continue"

Graves says that this level, besides being the seventh, is the first level of another set of levels. Once we have solved the problem of being one with others, we start the mechanisms that move man to a level where, for the first time, it is possible to see a major difference between man and other animals. The difference is that man attains a global point of view in all that he does, and he is certain that he must take action to create change in society.

Those are the seven levels of personality and values expressed by Claire Graves. When you need to do the type of work that involves, for example, making deep changes in a person's personality, you will need to make changes in his core values. Major personality shifts often require making major changes in values. It is important to make sure that the model you are using is the same as theirs. Using the Graves System, you can assist your client to make the transition more easily from level to level. Of course, you will want to get both conscious and unconscious approval and define the goal or outcome for making the changes.

19

Resolving Beliefs and Values Conflicts

Now I want to move this section toward completion with some work that Robert Dilts has done in terms of beliefs and values. He believes that most major health problems are in part a result of beliefs or values conflicts inside the individual. In his NLP therapies, Dilts is able to make major health changes and seemingly miraculous cures by making simple beliefs, value shifts and integration.

In terms of health, the question is, what happens when people have cancer and they believe that cancer causes death? They die, right? Now, based on what you already know about memories and values, how would you then make a shift in a person's beliefs and values?

The first step is to elicit their beliefs and values. Here are the steps in a values elicitation:

STEPS IN VALUES ELICITATION

1. Ask: **what's important to you about** _____? (The blank could be any contextual modifier, like relationships, working, your job, health, etc.)

2. Next, **number the Values according to their importance** (What is their value to you?) Ask:

   (a.) Of the above values, which is the most important to you?

   (b.) Assuming you have [list values already chosen], is _____ or _____ more important to you?

   (c.) Assuming you have [list values already chosen], if you couldn't have _____ but you could have _____, would that be OK?

3. **Rewrite the list of values according to their importance.**

4. **Elicit complex equivalents:** (To get the meaning of the words if desired).

   (a.) How do you know when you're _____?

   (b.) What does that mean to you?

   (c.) How do you know when someone _____ you?

   (d.) What is your evidence procedure for _____?

   (e.) What causes you to feel _____?

   5. **Elicit the submodalities** for the values that you want to work on.

Write down the actual words that you get from your client. The words themselves are important. Do not change them! Please just write down exactly what the person says. The words, whether positively stated or negatively stated, are how your client represents that particular value. ***Do not change the words.*** Do not ask your client to re-state the words so that they are stated positively. (We differ from Steve Andreas on this one point.* If you change your client's values so they are all positively stated, then you do not allow yourself to adequately map your client's model of the world. You are also putting your values on top of your client.) Just elicit the values as they are, and note in your own mind if they are toward or away from values (see "Meta Programs"). Toward and away from values on the same subject have the potential for conflict and may need to be resolved.

EXERCISE

Let's do an exercise with your values, OK? Try this: Think of what's important to you about your job. Write down eight things that are important to you about your job, and then number them according to their importance to you, with 1 the most important and 8 the least important.

YOUR VALUES

_____

_____

_____

Change Your Mind and Keep the Change, Steve Andreas, 1987.

_____

_____

_____

_____

_____

_____

SUBMODALITIES REVIEWED

The subject of submodalities is more than adequately covered in Richard Bandler's *Using Your Brain for a Change*, which we highly recommend, especially if you are just learning about submodalities for the first time. In any case, in working with a person, you want to discover the critical submodalities that are operative in giving meaning to the values. An example of this is knowing the difference in how they represent their number one value and their number ten value. Now, when you stop and consider that you have a special way to know that a certain value like "good relationships" is more important to you than "success," how does your brain do it? Well, the brain encodes the visual representations (the pictures) of your values differently so you know which is which. The way it encodes the differences is by changing the brightness, the color, the location, the motion and whether you see yourself in the picture (among other things).

EXERCISE

Now take your number one value, which you elicited earlier, and notice how you represent it. Do you have a picture? If not, make one. Look at the picture. Notice if it is:

Associated (through your own eyes) or Dissociated (seeing yourself)

Black and White or Color?

Focused or Defocused?

Near or Far?

Bigger than Life, Smaller or Regular Size?

A Movie or Still?

Is the Movement Fast or Slow?

Panoramic or Does it have a Border?

Does it have a Location?

Are the sounds:
  Loud or Soft?
  Fast or Slow?

Is there anything about the Pitch, Rhythm or Tonality? Are there any feelings?

Now do the same thing with the second value and notice that some of these elements are different in the second value. The elements that are different are the critical variables in YOUR storage of a value. The elements that you found to be different may not be the critical elements in someone else's storage of values. So if you are doing values change work with someone else, make sure that you elicit the submodalities of the pictures that represent the values.

Now, look at the values to see if you can spot any potential values or beliefs conflicts. Money and freedom are often in conflict in an individual because more money is often equated with less freedom.

FINDING CONFLICTS

To get close to value and belief system conflicts, you have to dig deeply, and the questioning process may take a lot longer than if you were simply doing a values elicitation. It may even seem to the client that you are badgering him. You may have to dig this deeply to get to the deeper values and belief conflicts. Get him to verbalize, so you and he can understand what the possible values conflicts are and so you have clearly in mind your client's model of the world.

SEEMING PARADOX

When you find a value and belief system conflict, you are likely to hear one of the following paradoxical statements. These are the red flags for value or belief conflicts:

The first is, "… Gee, I don't know what prevents me." Or they may say something like: "This may sound crazy, and it doesn't make any sense."

The second is, "This doesn't make any sense." What you're looking for is a paradox—"Something prevents me but I don't know what it is."

Third, "This just isn't like me."

Fourth, "I don't understand this, but…"

Fifth, "Logically I know this isn't true, but…"

Sixth, "I don't believe this, but…"

FOUR MORE FLAGS

As you get deeper and deeper in their values, you may get one or more of these flags. As they occur, they let you know that a conflict is occurring.

SMOKE SCREEN

The first impression is that of a smoke screen, where a person gets very vague or blanks out in order to protect himself from having to be in contact with his memories. For example, you will find that when a person was abused in his youth, major pieces of his memory are missing. When you take him back on his Time Line and you say, "… as you look back into the past," also ask, "… is your Time Line contiguous? Can you see the whole thing?" If there's a problem in this area, they'll say, "… no, there's a major chunk missing from age 5 to 7." That major chunk missing should be a red flag to you that there is a traumatic experience or abuse that occurred when he was a child.

Blanking out portions of memory in Time Line is the same thing as the smoke screen, where people blank out portions of their values in order to protect themselves from having to consciously deal with traumas. In each case they may be blanking out major portions of their memories.

BLIND ALLEY

The next one is the blind alley. The person may take you down a blind alley or give you misleading or irrelevant cues. Your client may tell you a long story. You discover, only after listening to the story for thirty minutes, that the story has no relevance to the presenting problem.

PROJECTION

Projection is often the hardest to detect. Projection is projecting your own beliefs and values on someone else. It is a major cause of the Mind Reading linguistic pattern.* (Mind Reading is when your client professes to know what someone else is thinking.) Of course there are two possibilities for Projection. One is the client. The other is you. So you might also want to eliminate any projection on your part.

A major belief may manifest itself in projection. For example, do you know anyone who is prejudiced? You see, prejudice is a result of projection. It is a values system that is built up at a very early age, probably in the Modeling Period. If you want to change it, go back and change the value that is a result of the imprint that occurred in the Socialization Period. To assist your client in overcoming prejudice, go back and discover what was going on from ages 14 to 21. The presenting problem is a result of those memories and decisions. If you change them and take them out you will get rid of the prejudice.

In the present, the reaction is to an earlier experience, i.e., "flashing back" to it. The person is reacting to an experience now that is a result of an experience that occurred earlier in life. Once someone is "set off" by something similar to the earlier occurrence, he usually is reacting to that previous experience.

For example, in a presenting problem of prejudice, you will want to know about the original experience that caused the

---

*See *Structure of Magic, I*

person to *become* prejudiced. There is probably a whole chain of events that, when re-fired or set off, will bring the experience of prejudice into the now. If you decide to take the original experience out of the Time Line, that process will probably delete the entire gestalt of memories and give the person more choices about how to react in the present.

The way to do that is to have him float above his Time Line, to go back and find the event and then to change or delete it. When you use the Time Line, you can take out the entire gestalt. (In memory a gestalt is like a chain of memories linking all the memories of a similar nature. "See Time Line".) Just take out the whole gestalt and it's gone. When you take out a memory, remember to replace it; otherwise it is likely to come back and may begin to regenerate itself. So be sure to have the client put another memory into his Time Line.

In some of these cases I erase or destroy the memory. In some cases I do not. It is just a judgment call. I guess the question is, can the person live with the memory or does it impinge on the now? If it does it would have been better to take out the memory. I always prefer to go for doing less and getting the most possible. That is, do less and accomplish more wherever possible. I do not want to take out more portions of a person's memory than I have to.

ABUSE

Take a case where there has been abuse. He may come to you because he just cannot remember his past. Often, somebody who has been abused will be thinking, "Gee, I've got whole chunks of things I can't remember. Why am I like this?" If you interview him about his Time Line, you'll probably find that major portions of his past are either dark or missing. That often signals an abuse case. He is going to say, "Why am I like this? Why don't I remember my past, and why don't I have any feelings in this particular area?"

So before you start working with abuse cases, by the way, you will want to tell him that you may dig up some memories that are unpleasant, and that it may require a period of adjustment before he is totally comfortable, or it may not. This is, of course, in the case of major trauma, where the kindest thing to do is to take all the memories out. Now, they may not want to take all the memories out; you always, therefore, want to get conscious and unconscious agreement that it's all right to proceed.

You can, if you wish, destroy the memory. Just have him run the full Phobia Model until the memory is gone. If you just run the Phobia Model once or twice you may not destroy the memory. More than three or four times will often destroy the memory. Fifteen times is almost guaranteed to destroy the memory. Just give the suggestion that, "... as you continue to run this, you may find it harder and harder to get the memory back, and I'd like you to continue to try until you can't get the memory back."

Some people will say they don't want to have you take the memories out. Then you can at least disconnect the feelings from the memories. (Use a temporal shift on the Time Line. See "Time Line".) The client will then be able to remember the memories without the negative emotions.

It's often kindest in an abuse case to take out the whole memory. He does not even have to be concerned about the pictures. One of the reasons he has come to you, as I said in the first place, is that he doesn't remember. He wants to know what happened. A lot of times it's better for him to know what happened, and because he does not remember, he may have assigned cause to the wrong person. This was very clear in the case of a woman who wanted to remember who it was who abused her. She was surprised and relieved to discover it wasn't her father, who she thought it was all those years. She was a lot better off when she discovered that her father was not the abuser.

MULTIPLE CAUSES

The fourth flag is multiple causes. This can be a sign that you are almost there as you identify a particular core belief or value system causing the situation. It is important to remember that a behavior is often caused by a complex interaction of a series of beliefs and values. So in order to handle that problem, you're going to have to find the trigger beliefs and values set that causes the behavior. Finding the trigger is much the same process as eliciting a strategy.*

WHEN YOU'RE CLOSE

Here are some other things that may occur. These things all help you identify when you are getting close to the major issues. When you find conflicts in beliefs and values, you may also find one or more of these four things:

1) **The Double Bind:** The Double Bind is a surface reflection of deeper beliefs and values conflicts. It's as if you are damned if you do and you're damned if you don't. For example, in a relationship, the wife says, "Why can't you be more spontaneous in our relationship, and why don't you bring me some roses sometimes?" The husband is in a double bind. If he brings his wife roses he cannot satisfy her, because she suggested it. So his trying will be met with more rejection.

2) **The Infinite Loop:** How about this one? "I can't do something new unless I've learned how to do it. But I can't learn how to do it until I do it." Do you know people like that? I do! And it is a clear sign of a beliefs and values conflict. By the way, this is also a sign of people who are afraid, and who are perhaps working up to a phobia. They cannot do something until they have done it before. So, you say, why don't you go downtown? "I can't, I've never done that before."

   "Can you help me back my car out of my parking lot?" a person asked me. "I said, "What do you mean, you've never backed your car out of the parking lot?" He said, "Yeah, but I've never backed it out of this parking lot before."

3) The next one is **Structural Logic:** This is like the infinite loop. I'm worthless because I can't do anything, and I can't do anything because I'm worthless.

4) The final one is **Paradoxical Behavior:** "I'm so concerned about being a bad driver that I make mistakes that put me in risky situations." You've seen it: people driving who are so cautious they almost get into an accident. (I believe that these

---

*See *NLP, Volume I*, Robert Dilts, et. al.

cautious drivers have formed a conspiracy and have decided to wait to leave work until just before I do, because they're always on the road when I am. This type of conflict may not be major, but it is annoying to me and it does suggest internal conflict. So let's get all overly cautious drivers into therapy immediately!)

CHANGING AND INTEGRATING VALUES

With all this in mind, we now have a basis for knowing what specific techniques to use to make changes in beliefs and values systems. The first one is the visual squash or spatial reframe.

Here's a story about values elicitation and the visual squash: I actually did this over the phone with an associate in Philadelphia, who said to me, "I am not making as much money as I think I really ought to make."

I said to him, "What's important to you about what you do?" (I asked that because "what you do" is the way that you earn money, isn't it?)

He said, "You're eliciting my values, aren't you?"

First I found his top eight values. The first value was freedom and the fourth was money. Now, to my way of thinking, that's the way it should be. He had money in there, so he should have been making money. So what was the problem?

If money was not there, I could have put it in the values hierarchy, using submodalities changes that we are about to describe. If money wasn't there, just putting it in the values hierarchy would change how he acts. But money was there, and I thought, "Well, that's interesting!" And I said to him, "So, the problem is that freedom is your highest value and you want to make more money. Is it that part of you wants to be free and part of you wants to make more money?"

He said, "Yes."

I said, "What I'd like you to do is to have the part that wants to make money come out, (pause) and which hand would that part like to be on?"

He said, "The right hand."

"I'd like the part of you that wants to be free come out and be in the left hand. I'd like to ask the freedom part, what is its intention, its purpose?"

He said, "Freedom."

"And what's the purpose of the money part?" I asked.

"To make more money, so I can have all the things I want so I'll be comfortable."

I asked this question, "For what purpose..." about five times, and finally he said, "... freedom, (pause) and my hands are moving together."

"Just allow them to continue," I said.

When his hands came together, he said, "Oh my God, my whole body is tingling and shaking. It's light!"

I said, "Great, the parts have integrated! Now, do you have a visual image of this new part that is in charge of freedom and money, allowing yourself to make as much as you want and yet retain your freedom?"

I couldn't see him because I was on the phone, but he said, "Yes." I said, "Good. We've created a lot of new behaviors today and I want you to make sure that your new behaviors are OK with all the other parts inside you. Could you just go inside and check and make sure they are OK?" He said they were, and we were done. Since we were on the phone, I said good-bye.

A month or so later, when I talked to him, he told me that about a week after we talked on the phone he had written a goal to have $10,000 invested in his business within a month, and that one week after that someone had walked into his office and asked to invest in his business. Amazing? No, not really—just the congruency that comes from handling deep internal beliefs and values conflicts. How do you do it? With a Visual Squash. So here are the steps in a Visual Squash:

Visual Squash

The Visual Squash is very important in changing and integrating a person's values and beliefs. Where there are incongruities or problems (even minor ones) there are usually internal parts conflicts. The Visual Squash will easily resolve conflicts between those parts and integrate them.

THE STEPS

1. **Identify the conflict and the parts involved.** Use values elicitation and other language patterns to sort out the values, beliefs and the parts that represent them.

2. **Ask each part to come out on one of the hands** Form (or discover) the visual image for each part. Describe each part. (It is much better if each part is described in "people" terms.)

3. **Separate intention from behavior.** (Reframe each part, chunking up so that he realizes that he has the *same* intention. See "Hierarchy of Ideas"—next chapter.) What resources does each part have that the other part would find useful in helping it to be more effective?

4. **Have each part tell you what is good about the other part.** And then have each acknowledge that the conflict is getting in the way of achieving their intention.

5. **Resolve the conflict** by getting agreement that they will work together. (If integrating, continue. If not integrating, end here.) Point out that they have a lot more in common than they realized and get agreement to integrate.

6. **Ask how they would like to integrate.** (Hands should move together; if not, help to collapse the image so that only the new part remains.) Then ask the person to describe the visual image of the new part.

7. **Take the integrated image inside.** (Also see "Changing the Basis of Personality", Appendix III.)

NEW PART DOES TIMELINE

Now, one of the things that is very valuable in terms of making major paradigm shifts in people is that once you have a new "super" part, you take the new part back on the Time Line and make the necessary shifts in their personal history. You can shift beliefs and values, and integrate the parts, but it'll be much stronger if you go back and make a shift in the Time Line, too. This will handle the parts conflicts, and the history. If you haven't made the shift agreeable with the part that is responsible for maintaining these value systems, then the part may shift them back. And if you have forgotten to change or align the history, then the parts may shift back. So, have the new super part go back and make the shifts in the Time Line so that the history becomes consistent with the new belief. If you have a history that is not consistent with the parts, the change may regress.

You want to make the history in the past consistent with the new behaviors that are going to be generated by the new "Super Part," so have the part itself do the changes in the Time Line. That will make a major shift. We are talking here about major personality shifts, more than just a few values changes. Have your new Super Part go back and clean up the Time Line, then make sure you integrate the part. When you're done, have all the parts get around the center and give each other a hug and integrate as if they were one. If you have trouble getting the two parts to agree, the next chapter will help.

20

The Hierarchy of Ideas

If you've ever had any trouble getting two parts to agree, then this section will help you get the desired results. In addition, the "Hierarchy of Ideas" can be useful in negotiation and mediation.

Stop for a moment and consider that in the entire range of your thinking process your thinking moves through various levels or strata from ambiguous to specific ideas. Each idea, besides having different content, is also different from the other in its degree of specificity or ambiguity. If you were to consider, for example, the idea of cars. (See diagram, next page.) Take cars as a notion. What an idea!

Let's call moving from specific to abstract "chunking up" and moving from abstract to specific "chunking down." If you take any idea in the universe, you can become either more specific about it or more abstract about it. So with the notion of cars, in order for me to get more concrete or more specific, i.e., in order for me to chunk down from cars, I will have to talk about classes and categories of cars or parts of cars. At some point in the hierarchy of ideas, as I move from abstract to specific, I have to talk about classes and categories or parts.

If I were to chunk down from cars into classes and categories, then I could talk about BMWs or Pontiacs or Porsches (i.e., any kind, class, category of car). If I were going to chunk down from Pontiac, then I would probably talk about the Pontiac Fiero, and if there were kinds of Fieros then we would probably talk about a GT. Notice that each level down gets more specific, and that the number of units in the category is smaller.

Let's chunk back up to cars now and look at the other way of chunking down. This time we are going to have to talk about

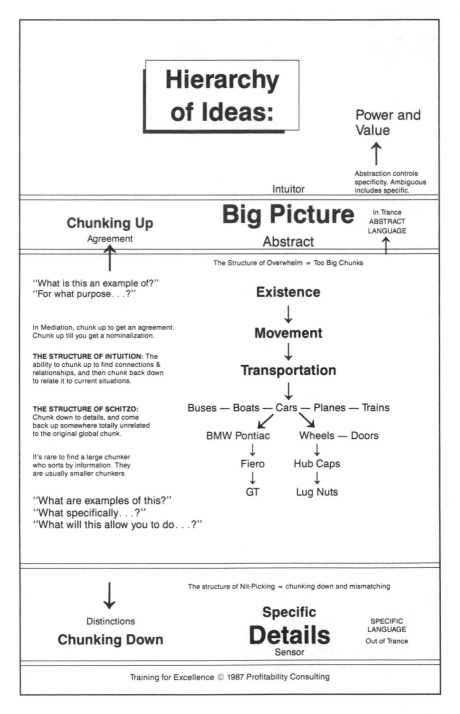

Hierarchy of Ideas:

Power and Value

↑

Abstraction controls specificity. Ambiguous includes specific.

Intuitor

Chunking Up
Big Picture   In Trance ABSTRACT LANGUAGE

Agreement

Abstract

↑

↑

The Structure of Overwhelm = Too Big Chunks

"What is this an example of?"
"For what purpose. . .?"

Existence

↓

In Mediation, chunk up to get an agreement. Chunk up till you get a nominalization.

Movement

↓

THE STRUCTURE OF INTUITION: The ability to chunk up to find connections & relationships, and then chunk back down to relate it to current situations.

Transportation

↓

THE STRUCTURE OF SCHITZO: Chunk down to details, and come back up somewhere totally unrelated to the original global chunk.

Buses — Boats — Cars — Planes — Trains

It's rare to find a large chunker who sorts by information. They are usually smaller chunkers.

BMW Pontiac   Wheels — Doors

↓   ↓

Fiero   Hub Caps

↓   ↓

"What are examples of this?"
"What specifically. . .?"
"What will this allow you to do. . .?"

GT   Lug Nuts

The structure of Nit-Picking = chunking down and mismatching

↓

Specific

Distinctions

SPECIFIC LANGUAGE

Chunking Down

Details

Out of Trance

Sensor

parts of cars. So if I wanted to talk about parts of cars, then I would talk about doors, fenders, wheels or antennas. Then, chunking down from wheels we would get hub caps. Parts that are smaller than hub caps are lug nuts. So we are looking at smaller parts or parts that are parts of the other. So at some point in the hierarchy of ideas, if you're chunking down you will have to decide if you want to talk about classes and categories *or* parts.

Let's chunk up from cars, now, and move in the direction of abstraction for a moment. If I wanted to talk about something more abstract than cars, I would ask myself the question: "What are cars an example of?" And, of course, I might come to the answer, "transportation." Do you notice something about what kind of word "transportation" is? You can't put it in a wheelbarrow. Now, "cars" you can put in a wheelbarrow. I guess you might have to have a LARGE wheelbarrow, but if you did you could put a car in there. Notice that no matter how large the wheelbarrow is, you can't put transportation in there.

So chunking up from "cars" I got to a word that is a function or process word, but the process has been fixed in time as it was turned into a noun. A process word that has been turned into a noun is called a nominalization. A nominalization is any noun that you cannot put into a wheelbarrow because of its abstraction.

Continuing to chunk up: What's transportation an example of? Movement. And in order to move, you must first exist. At some level of abstraction, in order to chunk up, you must use nominalizations.

Now, why worry about the Hierarchy of Ideas in the first place? Well, the answer is that we all communicate every single day. We all communicate with each other on a daily basis, and in the process of communicating some of us communicate more abstractly and some of us communicate more specifically. And if you are not speaking the same language as the other person then communication does not take place. We may *think* we're communicating when we say something like, "We've got to increase our communication!" And whoever you were talking to probably thought he knew what you were saying.

In other words, if you're too ambiguous with a concrete person, he is going to think you're talking fluff and that you never get to the point. They will think that you're pie in the sky and that you are not communicating because you do not have your feet on the ground. Whereas if you are talking too specifically for somebody who prefers the big picture or is abstract or ambiguous, he will think you have too many details and that you are boring. They are probably going to check out on you, because you didn't give them the big picture. And they may be turned off by the mountain of information that you have thrown at them.

In a recent training that we did for a branch of military intelligence, a Captain told us the following story. One day he got a call from an Admiral, who said, "I need information on the situation in the Middle East." The Captain prepared an excellent paper on the current political situation, the feelings of the people who live there and what was going on. The Admiral called back, "No, no, not that. I want to know how many battleships, how many destroyers, you know..." The Captain re-did his excellent paper. The next call from another Admiral asked for the situation in the Indian Ocean. The Captain prepared a paper on the current strength in the Indian Ocean, the number of battleships and so on. The second Admiral called back saying, "I wanted to know the political situation, not the number of ships!" The Captain then told us he thought the training on the Hierarchy of Ideas would save him countless hours in the future, because he would be able to discover in the future what level of abstraction was expected in his report.

So it's important in communication to be matching the kind of thought processes that are going on in the person you are talking to. That is, you want to match a person's level of thinking in the range of specific to ambiguous.

If you were to look at the notion of the Hierarchy of Ideas (page 194), how would you move from abstract to specific? How would you chunk down? There are two questions in the diagram. One thing you can ask yourself in your own mind is, "What are examples of this?" Let's go back to the notion of cars. Now, what are examples of cars? Pontiacs. What are examples of Pontiacs? Fieros. What are examples of Fieros? GTs.

The question, "What are examples of this?" doesn't always work, so there is another question, "What specifically?" (The entire Meta Model [see *Structure of Magic I and II* by Richard Bandler and John Grinder] is a tool designed for chunking down. And if you want to become a master of chunking, then learn the Meta Model.)

One of the problems often found in business and communication is that the person doing the communicating is chunking at a more abstract (or concrete) level than the person who is receiving the communication. This does not work, because if I begin to talk to you in phrases that are ambiguous, then you need to go inside and make up the rest of what I am saying. So, for example, if one of your workers comes up to you and says, "I'm sad," and you say, "Oh yeah, I really understand." Understand what? You understand the word sadness? How could you? In order for you to really know, you have to have the same experiences as your worker and you have to access them in the same way. You actually have to go inside and make up the meaning for the word sad. "About what?" is the question I would ask. "About what specifically?" This will increase your understanding and therefore your communication.

One of the other problems that occurs in communication is that people often fail to chunk up. Now, you might wonder, what is the purpose for becoming more ambiguous? Let me just suggest that, in the process of communicating and in the process of determining the importance of information, a very valuable procedure is to check the bigger picture. When I train people in communicating I also like to train them in the meaning of communication. It is important to train them in the meaning of what they are doing and how it relates to the bigger system, the ecology and the consequences of their actions. The question, "For what purpose?" is very important.

By the way, if you want to go in and heat things up in an organization, start asking, "For what purpose?" In an organization the purpose of any lesser structure is to serve the greater structure. The purpose of any part of an organization is to serve the greater whole of the organization. Similarly, the purpose of any class, category or piece of an organization is to serve the class, category or piece of the organization right above it. For example, the purpose of wheels is to serve the car. Wheels serve the car by getting it from place to place. But what happens from time to time in organizations is that the parts of the organization forget what their purposes are. They forget what their purposes are, and they begin to create purposes on their own that do not necessarily serve the organization. It's as if the wheels defined a new way to roll. "Don't bother me now. I'm on a new roll." It is as if they took on a life of their own. When dealing with organizations I'd like to suggest that you might want to keep in mind that the purpose of any lesser part of an organization is to serve the greater part of the organization. So any time that you have a question about parts of your organization, I would suggest that you ask yourself the question, "For what purpose?" "What is the purpose in my doing this?" "What is the purpose in this communication?"

The only way to find out if (or how) a lesser structure serves a greater structure is by the lesser structure asking, "What is the purpose?" or, "For what purpose am I doing this?" And that is the issue of chunking.

The question then becomes: how do you recognize abstraction or ambiguity in the people communicating with you and in yourself as well? Then, how do you help others in moving from the ambiguous to the specific? Conversely, how do you recognize specificity and how do you assist people in moving from the specific to the ambiguous?

The way you help people in moving from specific to ambiguous is to ask yourself the questions:

1. Of what is this an example?

2. For what purpose?

3. What's important to you about this?

Returning to the Hierarchy of Ideas as an example, ask, "Cars for what purpose? Transportation. What is transportation an example of? Movement. What is movement an example of? Ultimately it requires existence."

The Hierarchy of Ideas is also helpful in negotiation and mediation, which we will cover in a later book. Incidentally, there are many NLP techniques to help you in negotiation and mediation. Here is an example: If there are any two parts (or people, or pieces of an organization, or ideas) that disagree with each other (i.e., any two warring factions, as it were) you will find that if you chunk up by asking, "For what purpose?" enough times you will ultimately end in agreement as long as you are willing to go up as far as "existence." This is not a book on mediation. We train some of our students in specific mediation and negotiation techniques during the seminars we give. If we were to do a class on mediation, we might give you an exercise to assist you in using the technique of chunking in negotiation.

Regarding value and power, there is more power and more value in an abstract idea than in a specific idea. This is so because the more abstract idea controls the more specific idea. It controls the specific idea because it includes it. That is why the more powerful ideas often strike us in their simplicity. The connection between abstraction and value is also operative in how much people earn in an organization. A person's ability to move upward in the organization is dependent upon his ability to abstract or see the big picture. For example, in the Army, how much of the big picture does a Private see? How much of the big picture does the Sergeant see, versus the Lieutenant? How much detail do each of these people handle? Well, the Private handles all detail. The Sergeant handles fewer details. Guess how many details a General handles. Almost no details! The General has a Colonel or a Major to handle the details. So the Private handles almost all the details, and as you move up the hierarchy of rank, there are fewer and fewer details to handle up to the point where at some stage, which is roughly around the rank of Major, a military officer will have somebody to handle almost all of the details for him.

The same hierarchy is evident in an accounting firm. In an accounting firm, who puts the raw data into a journal? The journal entry clerk. The journal entry clerk is paid less than the bookkeeper who organizes the journal entries for the clerk and codes each piece of data. The bookkeeper knows which journal to put the entries into, but typically does not know how to prepare financial statements. The accountant knows how. But his boss, the CPA of the firm, who is paid the most, knows how to do everything everyone else does, and he also knows what the information in the financial statement means to the business. In an accounting firm, as in any business, the ability to abstract will determine how much a person is paid and how high he advances in a particular organization. You will notice that the higher-level people in almost any organization DO very little. That is their function.

The structure of intuition is the ability to chunk up and find connections and relationships and then to chunk back down and relate them to the current situation.

Here's one for you! The structure of "schizo" is chunking down to details and coming back up somewhere that is totally unrelated to the original big picture.

What is the problem in most communication? The problem is that the abstractions, while powerful, do not contain enough information for the person to be able to clearly grasp what is being communicated. In the process of communicating, an excellent communicator needs to move through all levels and all ranges of the hierarchy. This skill will give a person the ability to coach someone else who is being too specific or too ambiguous.

Why is chunking down to specifics important? It is important; because if the communication is too abstract, then the person receiving the communication has to hallucinate or make up the details. The problem in making up the details is that the details are often wrong!

So what we have provided here is a very elegant model showing how to get down to details or up into the loftiest abstractions so that you can recognize and communicate at whatever level is necessary! If you can get enough detailed information quickly and easily, while retaining the ability to fit it into the bigger picture, you have the ability to chunk up and down. Here is the true power in communication. It is in learning how to move through the entire range of the Hierarchy of Ideas and to reject neither abstraction nor specificity, but to be able to move through and be comfortable at any level. That is what the Hierarchy of Ideas is about.

21

Changing Values

ETHICAL CONSIDERATIONS

Next, let us take up some important ethical considerations about shifting a person's values. Following that, we will cover the procedure for changing values. Ethical considerations about changing values stem from the beginning of time. The question has been debated throughout the history of mankind. Different groups of people have wanted to change each other's values forever. As long as changing people's values has been a consideration, there have been ethical questions about it.

Of course, the issue of values does not come up unless and until someone else's values are different from yours. However, the question you should consider in evaluating values is not whether a person's values are different from yours, but whether his values hierarchy has conflicts. Does the hierarchy as arranged produce results? If the values hierarchy does not produce the desired results, then I believe that we have the responsibility to change it. The client has told us that he has a problem. The client has come to see us and asked our advice as an expert. Therefore, from this point of view, we have the responsibility to assist him in whatever way we can.

In addition, it is important to remember that people change their values all the time. Take the United States, for example. We've had some major value shifts in this country since the Vietnam War. All the hippies and yippees of the '60s and '70s have MBAs and drive Mercedes. People go through values shifts all the time. Of course, we have just made a gross generalization, but take work, for example. If you go to work for a group of people who are vegetarians and you love and admire them greatly, you will probably become a vegetarian. It happens all the time.

People shift their values all the time to adapt to their environment and to develop rapport with other people. Since the case is that values shifts are quite normal and usual, the issue of changing a person's values hierarchy becomes merely an issue of your client having what he wants in life. In that case, we are inclined to support the issue of entering into and changing somebody's values hierarchy.

We can make major short-term shifts in behavior by using the basic NLP techniques. One of the problems in NLP is getting long-term shifts in behavior. Our opinion is that longer-term shifts in behavior come from major changes in the belief and values systems that are the basis and cause of those behaviors in the first place. For example, we can shift somebody's behavior by giving him a new strategy. But if the strategy opposes the history (memories), then the change will not be as effective, or it may change back. Chaining anchors is a way of giving people new states and therefore new behaviors; but will those behaviors last? If they are accompanied by values and beliefs integration and hierarchy changes, they will last much longer than if values are not taken into account.

If, for example, somebody says, "I procrastinate," well, great, give him a new strategy by chaining anchors. That may or may not change the underlying cause. It may give him a new strategy and choices, while not handling the underlying beliefs, values or history that causes him to avoid using their resources in the first place. Ultimately they will still have the choice of procrastinating even if you have made these changes. If you want to make long-term shifts in people, you need to make major paradigm personality shifts. You need to change (a) the history that occurred and (b) you need to reframe the parts involved that maintain those behaviors. That is how to make lasting change.

We also believe that in changing the values hierarchy, the therapist should take into account the Hierarchy of Ideas and the level of abstraction that the various values hold in the Hierarchy. In the case of Values hierarchy design, the more abstract values should be higher than the more concrete values. At least, the highest value in the hierarchy should not be a concrete value.

Let us look at a hypothetical example. Assume you have a client who consciously and unconsciously wants to make more money. You elicit his values and find a #1 value of freedom and a #8 value of money. (See Example Hierarchy #1.)

Example Hierarchy #1:

Freedom

Communication

Good Working Conditions

Relationships

Growth

Meaningful Work

Group Consensus

Money

In this case, we suggest that moving money to the #1 value (which would replace freedom as the #1 value, moving it and all the other values down one) probably would not be right for our client. There are several reasons. First, money is not a value that is abstract enough. It is not even really a nominalization. Secondly, we know that some people who have money as a #1 value do not seem to be in balance. Thirdly, to move it from #8 to #1 in such a short time might be too much. So we would not make money into the #1 value. Perhaps changing money to the #2 value (see Example Hierarchy #2) would be a better idea. Just on the surface, with the hierarchy we have elicited, money may not even fit here, since making it #2 puts it above good working conditions.

Example Hierarchy #2:

Freedom

Money

Communication

Good Working Conditions

Relationships

Growth

Meaningful Work

Group Consensus

Checking with the client, you may then find that making money the #3 value would be a better idea, at least until we see the effects of the changes. (See Example Hierarchy #3.)

Example Hierarchy #3:

Freedom

Money

Communication

Good Working Conditions

Relationships

Growth

Meaningful Work

Group Consensus

We believe that a well-formed values hierarchy should have a more abstract value at the top.

Given those ethical considerations, there is no reason why we should not feel comfortable about changing values. Just make sure that you have investigated the ecology, that you have asked the standard NLP Well Formedness, Achievable Outcome and Meta Model questions. As you design the intervention, remember that the changes you create at this deepest level are going to generalize to other areas of life. Make sure that the intervention you design will be ecological if it generalizes, or be sure to contextualize it so that it does not generalize.

22

Utilizing and Changing Values

Now, let's work with a values hierarchy. This is rather easy work. First, you discover the values hierarchy—that's step one. (You have already elicited your own values in an earlier chapter in this section.) Step two would be to utilize the values, if you desired. Step three would be to design a new values hierarchy if needed, and we covered that in the last chapter. Step four is to change the values hierarchy.

VALUES UTILIZATION

The importance of the elicitation of values in this context is that once you have elicited someone's values (and for this purpose, we are only interested in the words they use), you can use his top four or five values in a single sentence, and provide an undeniable motivator to him. By using someone's top values in a single sentence or a paragraph, you are giving him a powerful unconscious motivating compulsion that will propel them to ward the goal. This is so because values provide the kinesthetic push or drive behind our motivation strategies. They are the actual push. In other words, the kinesthetic (feeling) that causes the motivation strategy to be motivat*ing*, is the same kinesthetic (feeling) that comes from the visual (picture) of the value.

By feeding back someone's values to him in order of importance, you provide an undeniable motivator because of the kinesthetic push and because of the rapport you have established with them. For example, just suppose these are the business values you have elicited for your client, arranged in order of importance:

Results

Integrity

Success

Relationship

Money

You can then feed him back a sentence such as, "You know, Wyatt, in supporting our proposal, I am also committed to RESULTS and INTEGRITY, and realize that our SUCCESS depends on our ability to maintain our RELATIONSHIPS as we make MONEY." That sentence will be very motivating for your client.

VALUES CHANGE DEMONSTRATION

Changing values in this context is very simple. Once you know the values hierarchy in a particular context, you can change the values by making a simple submodality shift in the values. If the meaning of the words is critical to your client, be sure to elicit the meaning of the words, the complex equivalence of each word.

TRANSCRIPT OF VALUES HIERARCHY CHANGE

Tad: "Who would like to make more money? OK, let's do Marvin. As you do exercises and experiment on your own, one of the things that we suggest is to make sure that what you do is reversible, until you are sure of what you are doing. You can put it back. We are doing major shifts here. The important issues are: You want to know that you can do it, and you also want to know that you can shift back if you need to. These submodality shifts in the values hierarchy are very simple, so it's easy to put them back the way they were. "Marvin, what's important to you about what you do?"

Marvin: "Fun, freedom, it's exciting, it's always new, always learning something, experiencing stuff."

Tad: "Is new and learning the same as experiencing new stuff?"

Marvin: "Yeah."

Tad: "OK. Is adventurous the same as new and learning?"

Marvin: "Yeah."

Tad: "What else?"

Marvin: "It's exciting."

Tad: "OK. Now, by the way, I don't know if you've noticed this, but when you do a values hierarchy elicitation, you'll probably get four or so, right off the bat—one, two, three, four. This is standard. Then what you're going to get is four more. What you want to do is make sure you get to the second level of four. Now it might be three and it might be five, whatever. Make sure you get to the second level, because oftentimes number one or two is in the second level of four. Notice what you just saw with Marvin; he just went one, two, three, four, then he stopped. He went "Ahhhh". Now he's going to remember four more here real quickly and he's going to give 'em to us."

Marvin: "I can meet new people, travel, live good and stay happy."

Tad: "You know what I just heard? Live good, stay happy sounds like parents' values that just popped up. When you say that inside your head, "live good, stay happy," do you hear your own voice come out?"

Marvin: "Yes."

Tad: "That's good. Fortunately there's no one else in there. What else is important to you about what you do?"

Marvin: "... staying active."

Tad: "What else is important? See, as long as I'm on a roll, I'm going to get a few more if I can. But I haven't got anything about money yet, have I? You're not going to work with money. Is money important?"

Marvin: "Yeah." (Tone of voice is rather uninspired.)

Tad: "I don't think I have ever heard anything so important to you, Marvin. (pause) Would you do it if you didn't get paid?"

Marvin: "Would I do it if I didn't get paid?"

Tad: "If you had all the other things, but you didn't make any money would you still be doing what you do?"

Marvin: "Yes."

Tad: "See, we want to know: what are the means values and ends values for Marvin? For Marvin, money's a means value. For some people money is an ends value, and it's important to know which it is for the person. Yeah, we can tell that money is going to lead to other things, and what we want to know is what that will lead to. But anyway, let's play a little bit, Marvin. (Pause) Of all these values we have here (showing him the list), what's the most important to you?"

MARVIN'S LIST OF VALUES (in the order elicited):

Fun

Freedom

It's Exciting

New Learning, Experiencing, Always New

Meet New People

Flexible

Travel

Live Good

Stay Happy

Staying Active

Money

Marvin: "The most important to me is to stay happy."

Tad: "OK. Is staying happy more important to you than being exciting?"

Marvin: "Yes."

Tad: "More important than learning?"

Marvin: "Yes."

Tad: "More important than meeting new people?"

Marvin: "Well, they're somewhat the same, I think."

Tad: "So they're the same?"

Marvin: "As stay happy."

Tad: "Stay happy is more important than what? Is stay happy more important than stay active?"

Marvin: "Yes."

Tad: "More important than flexible?"

Marvin: "Yes."

Tad: "More important than money?"

Marvin: "Yes."

Tad: "So stay happy is number one? (Pause) Of these values, what is the next most..."

Marvin: "Fun."

Tad: "Is fun more important than freedom?"

Marvin: "Yes."

Tad: "Is it more important than staying active? More important than being flexible?"

Marvin: "Yes."

Tad: "More important than money?"

Marvin: "Yes."

Tad: "What's the next most important value to you?"

Marvin: "Exciting."

Tad: "Is exciting more important than freedom?"

Marvin: "Yes."

Tad: "More important than meeting new people?"

Marvin: "Yes."

Tad: "More important than travel?"

Marvin: "Yes."

Tad: "More important than living good?"

Marvin: "Yes."

Tad: "More important than staying active?"

Marvin: "Yes."

Tad: "More important than being pleasant?"

Marvin: "Yes."

Tad: "Freedom more important than money?"

Marvin: "Yes."

Tad: "Exciting more important than money?"

Marvin: "Yes."

Tad: "Assuming you had stay happy, fun, exciting, what's the next most important value to you?"

Marvin: "Learning."

Tad: "So, if you were learning and you had no freedom then it would be OK?"

Marvin: "Yes."

Tad: "Is it more important than meeting new people?"

Marvin: "Yes."

Tad: "More important than travel?"

Marvin: "Yes."

Tad: "More important than living good?"

Marvin: "Yes."

Tad: "More important than staying active?"

Marvin: "You bet."

Tad: "More important than flexible?"

Marvin: "Um hmm."

Tad: "More important than money?"

Marvin: "Yes sir."

Tad: "OK. OK. Uh, assuming you had stay happy, fun, exciting and new learning, what's the next most important value to you?"

Marvin: "Freedom."

Tad: "Is that more important than meeting new people?"

Marvin: "Yes."

Tad: "More important than travel?"

Marvin: "Yes."

Tad: "More important than living good?"

Marvin: "Yes."

Tad: "More important than staying active?"

Marvin: "Yes."

Tad: "More important than flexible?"

Marvin: "Two of them are somewhat the same."

Tad: "Freedom and flexible are the same? Which is more important?"

Marvin: "Being flexible."

Tad: "More important than money?"

Marvin: "Yes."

Tad: "OK. Flexible is more important than meeting new people?"

Marvin: "Yes."

Tad: "More important than travel?"

Marvin: "Yes."

Tad: "More important than living good?"

Marvin: "Yes."

Tad: "Staying active?"

Marvin: "Yes."

Tad: "More important than money?"

Marvin: "Yes."

Tad: "Is it more important than being flexible?"

Marvin: "Yes. (Pause) Flexible?"

Tad: "Just kidding. Just kidding. OK. So what we've got is the top six values. So if I said, "Marvin..." looking at these in order, "... staying happy, fun, exciting, new learnings, freedom and flexible."

Marvin: "That sounds like about it."

MARVIN'S LIST OF VALUES (in order of importance):

1.	Stay Happy
2.	Fun
3.	It's Exciting
4.	Learning, Experiencing, Always New
5.	Freedom
6.	Flexible
Values	Meet New People
below #6	Travel
were not	Live Good
ranked	Staying Active
	Money

Tad: "OK. What we said was that what we want to do is to make more money. Is it OK with you to change the relationship of money in this hierarchy?"

Marvin: "Oh, yes, in fact, considerably."

Tad: "I'm not sure how it will change, yet, for the moment, so if (pause) I just want to make sure it's OK with you; if not, then we can put it back. So we'll put it there and see how it feels, or feel how it sees."

Marvin: "Right."

Tad: "And this works. Let's check it out. Um, so when you think about staying happy..."

Marvin: "Um hmm."

Tad: "Is it a picture?"

Marvin: "Um hmm."

Tad: "Is it in black and white or color?"

Marvin: "Color."

Tad: "Is it, uh, bright or dim?"

Marvin: "It's bright."

Tad: "How unique. Does it have a location?"

Marvin: "Um hmm."

Tad: "Where is that location? Center and...?"

Marvin: "Off center and a little off to the right."

Tad: "Center, right. OK. Does it, uh, have a border around it?"

Marvin: "Yes."

Tad: "What is the color of the border? Is there a color in the border?"

Marvin: "No it's black."

Tad: "Is it a still or a movie?"

Marvin: "Motion picture."

Tad: "Is it focused or defocused?"

Marvin: "Focused."

Tad: "OK. When you think of... put that picture aside for a moment (pause) when you think of money, do you, uh, see a picture?"

Marvin: "Hmm, sort of."

Tad: (To the room) "Can you see the difference? Already he's got a major difference. He "sort of" has a picture! So that sort-of picture, is it... what is it? Is it focused or defocused? How come you can't see it now, what I'm asking?"

Marvin: "Uh, because it fluctuates in and out of my mind."

Tad: "How does it fluctuate in and out of your mind? (pause) Pictures?"

Marvin: "The pictures change."

Tad: "The picture's changing? Are you seeing money or what it can get you or... but the pictures keep changing?"

Marvin: "Oh, it fluctuates between money and..."

Tad: "And staying happy doesn't fluctuate?"

Marvin: "It does, but not as rapidly. I have different pictures of being happy."

Tad: "So, the fluctuation is faster?"

Marvin: "And it's a still."

Tad: "Oh, and there are a bunch of stills."

Marvin: "Yeah. They kind of click."

Tad: "They kind of click? And they're in the what, lower quadrant?"

Marvin: "Yes."

Tad: "Is it, uh, black and white or color?"

Marvin: "Color."

Tad: "Right. Is it Color?"

Marvin: "I guess, yes."

Tad: "Is it a sort of a series of stills?"

Marvin: "Yes."

Tad: "In focus or defocused?"

Marvin: "It's focused."

Tad: "OK. Good. Now, just for the purpose of this exercise, what we're going to do is to change the submodalities of money, to the submodalities of to-stay-happy, and well, we'll see what happens. So I'd like to take money and bring it up on the screen. I'd like you to move it so that it is center right. Good. Now, bring it up so it's full color. Ok. And slow down the fluctuation so that it is at the same sort of fluctuating speed as staying happy. Put a black border around it. The same sort of border that was around staying happy. Uh, I'd like you to make it into a movie. Now, remembering the way money is, I'd like you to think of staying happy at the moment and is it, uh, associated or dissociated?"

Marvin: "Staying happy?"

Tad: "Uh huh."

Marvin: "It's both."

Tad: "What? How do you do that?"

Marvin: "Sometimes I'll see myself happy and sometimes through my own eyes."

Tad: "So when you think of money now, I'd like you to have that same process occur of (pause) going back and forth. I'd like you to leave that there for a moment, the way it is (pause) and now I'd like you to clear your screen. Now, as you think about what's important to you about what you do. OK? What do you think about money?"

Marvin: "Nice."

Tad: "And? Is money more important than fun?"

Marvin: "Yes, fun could have fun money."

Tad: "Is money more important than being exciting?"

Marvin: "Yes, you could probably do more exciting things with it."

Tad: "Is it more important than new learning?"

Marvin: "I could probably get more new learnings with money."

Tad: "So if we had to rate money somewhere in there..."

Marvin: "Well, kind of side by side..."

Tad: "So money has now become..."

Marvin: "It's like leverage."

Tad: "Like leverage? Now if I said I'd like you to choose, and tell me where it is in terms of your hierarchy, is it like number 1, 2 or 3? I mean, staying happy sort of makes you think, too, is this right up there with staying happy?"

Marvin: "It's more like right under it."

Tad: "Yes."

Marvin: "Somehow. All the other stuff comes along easily."

Tad: "Great. Now that's exactly what I expected to happen. When you take the submodalities of whatever value it is that you're putting up there, and make it the same as the number one value, it becomes a number two value. It wouldn't become a number one value unless you change the number one value's submodalities to another set of submodalities, or unless you took the number one value out of there, which I would hesitate to do.

"Typically, I've found that this particular shift is sufficient to have people remain with that value as their number two value (or whereever we put it) for long periods of time. It does not tend to shift back. It stays right there. So as you think about that, how's that inside? Good?"

Marvin: "Yeah."

Tad: "Tell me."

Marvin: "It's interesting because it was fluctuating between association and dissociation, and with me, money was always a dissociated thing, and it was like there was nothing to associate, to experience with. I didn't know what it meant, having a lot of money. And then I got memories of when I did have a lot of money, and really all of the positive financial stuff and lost most of the worry, and it feels good."

Tad: "Now, what's the difference between what we did here and the visual squash? Visual Squash is used when there's conflict. You see, if Marvin's parts did not agree with what we did, and there was a conflict between the money and the staying happy parts or any of the other values, what we would do is do a visual squash and integrate the two. After you've done the shift, if it shifts back then there's an internal conflict. In Marvin's case, when you have major values or belief conflicts, you use a Visual Squash, it's as simple as that. We did this quickly and the whole process took twenty minutes. We've made a major values shift in Marvin in twenty minutes."

QUESTIONS

Participant: "When you're eliciting the list of values and you sense a conflict, would you do just a simple values shift or would you do the squash instead?"

Tad: "I would have started with the Visual Squash and then done the submodality shift afterward, once I had checked the congruency of the parts integration."

"Now say that there's a conflict between several parts regarding the freedom and money values that we pick up. You're going to have to integrate them all. Keep doing the Visual Squash until you get them all integrated, until you get one part that is in charge of freedom and money. Remember that when you're dealing with someone's values, and he doesn't use the same words that you do, that doesn't mean that his values are different. If you want to find out what those words mean, you need to elicit the complex equivalents."

Changing The Basis
Of Personality

THEORY

Who we are is a result of our collection of memories, our values and beliefs and the parts that maintain them. Any incongruities, inability to get things done or health problems are a result of basic-level, core-parts conflicts. In addition, there are parts responsible for maintaining values and values hierarchies inside the individual. Finally, our personality is based on the collection of our memories and the templates of perception that are a consequence of significant events in our past.

THE MODEL

1. **INVESTIGATE – GATHER INFORMATION:** Meta Model, Keys to an Achievable Outcome, Presuppositions, Ecology

2. **FIND PRESENTING PROBLEM:** Presenting problem is the problem that the client presents to you as you begin the therapy. At this time you may also want to find the causal problem, although it is not absolutely necessary.

3. **PRESENT MODEL FOR CHANGE TO CLIENT:** (the language used is intentional) "A lot of things underlie other things, and sometimes when we do something, what we do is based on a belief that we have. Everything we do is a response to a situation, and so change is very easy, and

frequently when we change something fundamental, as we are going to do today, everything in life changes. Sometimes when we dig up a weed, we find one root, or sometimes we find several roots that all go together to form the problem. So we can deal with all that easily by dealing anywhere in the system, since like a weed, everything is connected."

4. **INSTRUCT CLIENT TO GO TO THE CORE:** "We're going to go to the core belief or value that makes this possible."

5. **QUICK INFORMAL REFRAME:** "We're going to explore new ways of doing things that will still allow you to get everything you want; we're going to get you everything you want today and you'll discover how to get it more easily, and you'd like that, wouldn't you?"

6. **BEGIN COMMUNICATION WITH THE UNCON-SCIOUS:** "I'd like to talk to the unconscious mind..." (If necessary, set groundwork with hypnotic language: "Now, you know you have a conscious mind, and I know that you have a conscious mind. But one thing that many people don't know is that they also have an unconscious mind, and the unconscious mind is the part of the mind that is here, and it is really responsible for all that you do. And as I talk to the unconscious mind, there isn't really any need for the conscious mind to listen to me, because the unconscious mind will hear everything that it needs to hear here, and that's what we want (need) today. And I want the unconscious mind to comfortably and easily decide what the conscious mind can do while we talk. Let him go off somewhere while we talk. I want to know some things about him..." etc.)

7. **ESTABLISH SIGNALS:** "... and what helps me when I talk to the unconscious mind is to have signals that I can see easily set up so we can communicate more clearly. Now I know you've seen people unconsciously moving their heads up and down when they meant 'yes' and back and forth when they meant 'no.' And that's one easy, comfortable way to communicate. Or even the movement of a finger could mean 'yes,'

like this." (Grab finger and move it as a demo.) And the movement of another finger could mean 'no.' (Demo it.)

8. **SET UP PROBLEM:** "You know, I can guess what's the most important problem to you to change right now, but that's just me, and I want you to know that we can change that easily, and it probably would be useful, and yet that's just me. You, however, really know what's most fundamental, and what change will actually create the most powerful effect in the broadest area to completely transform the individual's whole life." (At this point you should be getting strong signals.) "So, you know what situation it is that's most important to the individual right now?" (Signal) "Great!"

9. **IDENTIFY THE FIRST PLAYER:** "Do you know which part it is that does the thing you're most concerned about?"

10. **TALK TO THE PART:** (Still include the unconscious mind.) "I'd like to talk to that part, and if that part could come out on the hand, and let me show the hand how the part could be the most comfortable here (taking hand and turning it over), now."

11. **DEMONSTRATE SIGNALS:** (See #7)

12. **ASK FOR PERMISSION TO CALL IT "PART #1":**

13. **IDENTIFY OTHER PLAYER:** (Still include the unconscious mind.) "Is there another part that is involved in this, or a part that is the reciprocal, you know, the opposite number, the flip side of the coin?"

14. **DEMONSTRATE SIGNALS:** (See #7)

15. **TALK TO THE OTHER PART:** (Still include the unconscious mind.) "I'd like to talk to the other part, and if that part could come out on the hand, and let me show the hand how the part could be the most comfortable here (taking hand and turning it over), now."

16. **OPEN COMMUNICATION BETWEEN PARTS:** "Can you introduce yourself and tell Part #1 what your behaviors

are, what you do, how you do it, and what you hope to accomplish with that ([optional] because you know that every behavior is a response to a situation), and so what is it that you're actually doing? What is the ultimate purpose of these behaviors?" (Pause)

17. **CHUNK UP:** "And as you realize the purpose, what does that in turn do for the individual?"

18. **DO THE SAME FOR PART #1:** (Follow steps 15 – 16 for Part #1.)

19. **CHUNK UP AGAIN:** "Now, both parts, noticing what purpose that serves, and in turn what purpose that serves, chunk up, continuing to go up the hierarchy of logic until you can clearly see, hear and feel that your ultimate purpose, your values, are really quite similar (pause), if not identical (pause), even exactly the same." (Get yes signal from both.)

20. **ACKNOWLEDGE SAMENESS AND TELL IMPLICA-TIONS:** "You know, there is quite a lot of (complete) similarity in your intentions, beliefs and values." ([Optional when not integrating parts, only getting agreement:] "I propose an alliance that might be useful to both of you.")

21. **INTEGRATE AND PRESERVE:** "I'd like to suggest that since there's so much similarity between you that you be-come as if one, that you become one and preserve the good intentions, wisdom, skill and power that you each have, becoming more powerful as you do to achieve your inten-tion. Integrate and become 1,000 times more powerful." (Signal, hands move together.)

22. **CALL FOR OTHER PARTS:** "As you are realizing this, you may also begin to notice that you were really just two pieces of what once was a complete whole. (Signal) I'd like you to realize what other pieces of the original whole are missing and bring them forward and put them here." (Suggesting the space between or on top of the hands.)

23. **GET AGREEMENT FOR ALL PARTS TO INTEGRATE:** "Now, I'd like to have everybody introduce each other,

and… "(going to 15) "… until you see, hear and feel that your purposes are the same."

24. **THE POOL OF LIGHT:** "I want you to go inside and find the pool of light that exists inside in your center: you may have not even been aware of it until I mentioned it, and I want you to have the parts jump into it. Notice that the pool is pure light and energy, and pure love. It is your own pure essence. Bring it out here (outside the body). Now, as the parts jump in, watch them dissolve and become one with the light, (stop talking about parts) and draw this love, light, energy and any other good you need inside the body. Allow your hands to bring the light inside, into your center only as fast as it integrates into the center and watch… (pause) as the light goes out to all parts of the body, (pause) and the body becomes hollow (pause) as the light expands, expands, (pause) expands, (pause) expands to infinity. (pause) Notice that the entire universe is contained inside your body (pause) and that you are the universe. (pause) Now bring it back. Into your body. Make the light into the most useful shape that the new part will be, someone who has the characteristics of what you want your new part to be."

25. **FIND TIME LINE ORGANIZATION:** "Now what I'd like you to consider is how you store time. How do you, for example, know the difference between your memories… How do you know if you're looking at a memory or an event that is going to happen in the future? Because I'd like you to notice… Can you recall a memory from when you were age five? Notice where that came from. Good. Can you imagine what it's going to be like five years from now, or what will you be doing a year from now? Can you imagine that? Good. What direction did that come to you from? Over there? Good. So what I'd like you to notice is that your memories are arranged, for want of a better term, it's sort of a line that stretches from your future through now all the way to your past, and if you could float a little above that line, could you look down on the entire continuum of past, present and future so that you are seeing all your memories arranged in

that line? Can you do that now? Do you notice the entire continuum of past, present and future?

IF PROBLEMS HERE: "OK, I know there's a part of you that likes to do this and a part of you that thinks perhaps you shouldn't be doing it, and I think that's OK, and I'm wondering if the part that THINKS it doesn't want you to or THINKS you shouldn't be doing this is willing to play, explore and discover new ways of achieving its intentions while still allowing you to do this. Could you float above your time line now? I want you to tell that part that it's all right, that you've done this before and that it's really a simple procedure. And it increases choices and allows parts to achieve their intentions easier, far more easily than they had before this. And if it doesn't want to do that, perhaps it can do it just for purposes of this experiment. Can you do that? OK.

26. **HAVE THEM FLOAT ABOVE THEIR TIME LINE:** "Good. Excellent. Now, do you notice that all those events form sort of a line in your mind? Excellent. Very good. Very good. Now what I'd like you to do is to imagine that you're looking down on the events that form your past, present and future, as you float up above all that, so just sort of pretend that you're floating and that you're floating right up above your Time Line. And notice how good it feels to be above all that, that you can look down on the entire continuum—past, present and future. Very good. Excellent. Excellent."

27. **NOTE THE SUBMODALITIES:** Ask him to notice the Submodalities (SMDs), and make sure that the client's experience is that SMds are similar for the past, present, and future. It's OK and quite usual for the future to be brighter than the past. It's not good; it's unusual if there are black holes or missing pieces in the past. If the Time Line is not contiguous regarding the SMds, then change the SMds so that they are the same brightness and approximate color.

28. **GIVE THEM AN EXPERIENCE OF POWER OVER THE TIMELINE:** "And as you do that, I'd like you to go

back on your Time Line to an earlier time, and I'd like you to recall a pleasant memory... when you were much younger, somewhere between the ages of eight and 13. I'd like you to recall a pleasant memory. And I'd like you to notice that the memory has the same characteristics as... any other picture you make in your head, or any other value or belief. I want you to notice that the construction of the memory is exactly the same as anything else. And now I'd like you to float up above it all and feel good being above it all. Leave that memory behind for a moment and float up above your time line again and come forward to an age more than 21; more than age 21 and less than now, and I'd like you to take an unimportant memory. I'd like you to take a memory that doesn't matter, and I would like you to take that memory out of your time line. I want you to make sure that this memory has absolutely no significance, it doesn't matter, and that you can take it out of your time line. I'd like you to take that memory out of your time line and push it far away from you. I'd like you to push it further and further and make it darker and darker so that it becomes a little dot, and now push it into the sun and watch it blow up. Now I'd like you to take that memory or that space, actually, where the memory was, and fill it with something that matters, something that makes you happy. Perhaps it's a funny time or a time when you felt good about yourself. Or a time when someone else felt good about you. And make it so you smile. So you feel good about it. Excellent. And now I'd like you to come forward to now. Take as much time as you need to complete that before you come forward to now. And when you're at now, I want you to look forward into the future. Notice how far your time line extends into the future. And I'd like you to go out into the future all the way, but not quite to the end of your time line, and when you do that I want you to turn around and look back. Look back toward now so that the entire continuum— future, present and past stretch out toward you like a line. And I want you to notice as you look back from the future to now to the past, I want you to notice if there are any events there between the future and now that shouldn't be there or that you would prefer weren't going to happen. Just like the event you changed a moment ago. You can also manage the memory of the future in the exact same way. I'd like you to make sure that all the events between now and the future, as you look back from the future to now, support you. Support you in becoming the kind of person you want to be. Support you having the happiness and those things that you deserve. I want you to make sure that all those events in the future are of your creation and are those things that help you be the fullest person you can possibly be. And if there are any events in the future that you particularly want, I'd like you to pick one right now.

Pick an event in the future, something that you want to have happen. Move right up to that event, something that you really want, and I'd like you to look at that event in the future, and I'd like you to notice if that event in the future is something that is really compelling, that is, is it something that is really compelling you, something you really want? And what I'd like you to do is, I'd like you, for a moment, to step into the picture. See it through your own eyes, step into your own body and see what you'll see, hear what you'll hear and feel the wonderful feelings, and I want you now to turn up the brightness, make it sharper and more focused and closer, make it bigger, make it brighter, whatever you need to do, turn up the brightness on that picture so that it is the most compelling and make it even more compelling so that you really want it. So that you really, really want it. Excellent. Now, step outside of the picture so that you can see yourself. And put it in the future. Take all the time you need to complete this now, and come back now, float right back to now, and…"

29. **COME BACK TO CURRENT THERAPY:** "Now, every behavior is a response to a situation, and you know that situation we're dealing with."

30. **THE DECISION:** Have them go back into the past and find the earliest unwanted experience in the chain. "Find the first or most important time, the fundamental cause of the limits

as perceived by the conscious mind, and I want you to find the cause. I want you to go right to what makes this possible. There may be a certain mold that you decided to use long ago—a decision you made. You know, like a nozzle on a garden hose molds all the water that comes out, or like a cookie mold that molds the dough. Like a template. And like a template, a decision used by your unconscious molds all your perceptions and all your experience. Like that, I want you to find the decision that you decided to use long ago that is molding your experience. I want you to find the time you made the decision that is causing this problem. Do you find it?"

31. **CHANGE THE MEMORY USING CHANGE PERSONAL HISTORY, PHOBIA CURE MODEL, UNHOOK THE FEELINGS, OR JUST HAVE THEM REMOVE THE MEMORY:** If using the Phobia Cure Model, have them run the pattern until the memory is destroyed. Say, "I want you to run it until you can't get the memory back." What you say to the person, if you want that to happen, is much like the way you do the phobia cure, by presupposition. So what you would say is, as when you're doing a phobia cure, "I want you to run this until you can't get it back anymore." And he goes, "Oh, OK." And you say, "It might get harder and harder, but I want you to try to get it back." So he tries even harder, and eventually he won't be able to get the memory back. When you do the phobia cure on a memory over and over and over again, you will eventually destroy the memory so that it will be impossible to remember.

In some cases I erase or destroy the memory, in some cases I don't. It's just a judgment call. I guess the question is, can the person live with the memory, or does it impinge on present time? That won't work. In that case it would have been better to take out the picture. I'd always go for less for more, that is, do less and accomplish more wherever possible. I don't want to take out more portions of a person's memory than I have to.

You can have them take out a whole chain of feelings in the gestalt of the memory by just saying, "If you look in the lower right-hand corner of that picture, you notice that's where the feelings are hooked, you just unhook those feelings, you'll notice the feelings go away." I've had people drop off their feelings just by doing that.

32. **GIVE INSTRUCTIONS FOR GENERALIZATION:** After you destroy the memory you fill it with something new and you say, "I want you to look and notice that memories both before and after that have changed subsequent to changing this memory. Have you noticed that?" And they'll either say, "Yes," and you say, "That's right," but if they say "No," you'll say, "Good, we'll do it again, and it's probable that you just didn't notice; I'd like you to notice it this time." The changes will occur into the future from this particular memory that we're changing. So if you say it that way, they'll change the whole gestalt for you.

Now in the same way, when you put something out into the future, you make it very compelling. You also ask them to notice that they did change the events from now until the future simply by changing that memory. Now, it's my theory that it does. And they only have to notice it. It may also be presupposition. So what happens when you change the future memory is that it changes the whole chain of events going back to now. So when you work with the time line and you work with a single event, you're working with a gestalt.

33. **REPLACE THE DESTROYED MEMORIES:** If any memories have been deleted, replace them. "I'd like you to replace the holes we've created with new memories that only support your mastery of the new behavior, adopting new beliefs, values and attitudes that totally support your new behaviors."

34. **LOOP TO 32:** Continue steps 32-34 using the earliest memory available, until the unwanted state or behavior is not accessible.

35. **MAKE FIRM THE LEARNINGS:** What you've learned today "I'd like you to firm up. Keep them as something precious as a treasure, because that's what they are, and you know it."

36. **PAST PACE NEW BEHAVIOR:** Take the new desired behavior and put it in the past, having been performed as many times as necessary. "I'd like you to imagine having done this behavior as perfectly as possible at least 25,000 (as many times as appropriate) times in the past."

37. **FUTURE PACE AND TEST:** "I'd like you to uncover all those events that you buried in the future that no longer support the new you and get rid of them." Replace with new future memories. Make sure that there is a liberal sprinkling of new memories in the future that support the new behavior. "I'd like you to imagine using these new behaviors even into the future, and even as the content of your experience changes, these new supporting behaviors remain operative."

38. **CHECK ECOLOGY:** "Now, we've made a lot of changes today and generated many new behaviors. I want you to make sure that they are all right with all the parts inside."

39. **COME BACK TO NOW:** Have them float down back into their time line and come to now.

Cocaine Therapy

This is a transcript of a therapy with Tad and a client whose presenting problem was a $100-to-$300-per-day cocaine habit. We do not regard this as a particularly elegant therapy. It is included because the therapy got the intended produced results, and as an example just what a client might say. In the process of discovery, using standard NLP Well Formed-ness Condition techniques of specifying outcomes, it was also discovered that the client had dyslexia. (Portions of Tad's transcript are analogically marked out as being either louder or emphasized in a certain way. In transcribing the tape, we have emphasized those shifts in boldface type.) In this therapy, Tad was joined by Mark Wadleigh (a Master Practitioner and one of Tad's students) and the client's sister.

Greg: "If I could read all the jokes in *Playboy* in fifteen minutes, then I would know that my dyslexia was gone."

Tad: "Well, if I were reading *Playboy*, it wouldn't take me fifteen minutes, it'd take me a lot longer than that, but I'll tell you one thing, I wouldn't just be reading the jokes. (Laughter) So, maybe that'll be our test... (Pause) Greg, you have been on and off cocaine for a while. You quit three months ago and then you started back up again. And you want to get off it now? Is that right?"

Greg: "Yes."

Tad: "OK. So I want to start by asking you, you said [on our questionnaire] that you thought the future and the past were sort of up to down for you?"

Greg: "Oh yeah."

Tad: "Now, uh, so point to where the future is for you in terms of your memories or your memories of the past. Where's the future?"

Greg: "Where's the future for me?"

Tad: "Yeah. Yeah."

Greg: "Kinda like, I'd go like that." (Points up and in front of him.)

Tad: "OK. And where's the past?"

Greg: "I pointed down, but I'd like to point back."

Tad: "So, it's sort of behind you?"

Greg: "It's behind me, yeah."

Tad: "OK. **Now.** Can you just sort of imagine floating up above your entire continuum of past, present and future, so that you are almost looking down on the whole Time Line of your memories?"

Greg: "Yeah. Oh, yeah."

Tad: "OK. Do that now, float right up above that Time Line, just go right up there so that you're looking down, and do you have a sense of the entire line—past, present and future?"

Greg: "Pretty close."

Tad: "Now, let me ask you a question. The stuff that's in the past, is the brightness pretty much the same all the way through, or are there dark spots?"

Greg: "Yeah, it's like dark spots."

Tad: "There are some dark spots and dark areas?"

Greg: "Yeah."

Tad: "Are there areas that are missing... where there's nothing there or just dark spots?"

Greg: "Yeah, there's an area there where there are a couple things that are missing."

Tad: "All right. Uh. What age does that look like to you?"

Greg: "Oh, uh. It looks like 1972, whatever that would mean."

Tad: "And how old are you now?"

Greg: "Thirty-seven."

Tad: "So that would be uh, OK, about twenty-three."

Greg: "Yeah. Somewhere around there."

Tad: "All right. Um. What I'd like you to do is float high enough above your Time Line now, and I want to do a couple of experiments. One is I'd like you to see if you can sort of straighten it out so it's a line, because remember it was sort of at an angle, and I'd like you to just straighten that out so it's a **nice straight line**. (Pause) And then I'd like you to turn it. Actually rotate the line so that it is, uh, parallel to you."

Greg: "How about like that?" (Gestures)

Tad: "That's what it's like. Good job. (Pause) Can you float right down into it so that the line is right a..."

Greg: "Right about here?" (Gestures)

Tad: "At that level, yeah, that's right. (Pause) Now open your eyes. (To an observer) What I didn't tell you, Mark, is that Greg is highly intuitive, in case you hadn't noticed. (To Greg) How does it feel with your Time Line arranged that way?"

Greg: "Kinda strange. I feel almost like, you know when you're kids when you spin each other around. And you stop, and you go like this? (Demonstrates spinning) OK. I'm about there where it's like settling down."

Tad: "OK. So, you know just the minute you stop spinning, like when you were a kid, it took a couple of seconds or a few minutes to..."

Greg: "Yeah."

Tad: "Just get comfortable."

Greg: "Right."

Tad: "What I'd like you to do is **leave it there**, uh, and um, I want to talk about a few other things, and then I want to ask you some questions. So, right now it's still arranged like that? (Gestures)

Greg: "Yeah. I'm like this."

Tad: "Good. Which way is your past, by the way, since you've arranged it?"

Greg: (Gestures)

Tad: "So, you arranged it so your past is off to your left. So, good. Past. Good. Well, that's the way it wants to stay. It wants to stay right there like that. For the purposes of what we're doing with this."

Greg: "OK."

Tad: "You've heard these questions before." (Asks a series of questions to determine Myers-Briggs, Judger-Perceiver category.)

Greg: "You know that causes a hell of a vibration on this side, you know (Gestures to head)."

Tad: "Having your Time Line (h)over there?"

Greg: "The questions make me feel like going, 'whir', 'whir.'"

Tad: "With your... Let's see. Your future's over there, right?"

Greg: "Yeah."

Tad: "I see. So, you, your future says it wants to flip up there like that?"

Greg: "Yeah. It's like, a, you know, like fluctuates. Depending on the questions, you know, on things staying a little stable and 'woo', 'woo.'"

Tad: "Yeah. I noticed it was, uh, I sort of thought I noticed that."

Greg: "You know, like holding out a long stick, like a willow and 'rattatat.' Yeah."

Tad: "Right. So how does it feel in terms of **staying that way?** Do you feel OK, like you're going to be able to **stay that way?** Or will there be some question about it bouncing around, or is it going to **stay there?**"

Greg: "It feels like, I don't know. I can't answer that. I couldn't answer and say, yes or no, confidently 100%."

Tad: "Well, you know one of the things we talk about..."

Greg: "It's comfortable."

Tad: "Good, well that's good. One of the things we talk about in, uh, this kind of, uh, thing that we're doing, called Neuro Linguistic Programming, is that we talk about the question of who's driving the bus. You know a lot of people, uh, run their brains, uh, well, um, it's like when you buy a TV set they give you an owner's manual, right? But when you got your brain, they didn't give you an owner's manual.

Greg: (Laughter) "OK. I don't know if I got me a Ford or a Chevy. Is that what you're telling me?" (Laughs)

Tad: "Right."

Greg: "OK."

Tad: "You just sort of checked in there and nobody told you how to run it, and um, so, you know. The brain is an interesting thing because it'll do whatever it wants to do unless you give it something to do. You know what I mean?"

Greg: "Yeah. Oh, yeah."

Tad: "So what we're doing here is we're giving it something to do, and showing people they can have their brains under control. They can get their brains under control, and be able to run them themselves. We have. (Laughter) We have done that!"

Greg: "All right."

Tad: "You made a major shift."

Greg: "I can tell (Laughs)."

Tad: "And I'm sure you can tell him, from the inside, uh, and I think the important thing is making sure that those shifts are going to, uh, **want to be OK with that**. And that the, uh, the internal, shall we say, parts of you that are responsible for maintaining your collection of your memories, (Pause) see, you've got a way, I mean you must have a way, we all do, uh, of how to know which is the past and which is the future, 'cause otherwise, you'd just stick your memories in there and you wouldn't know which was which. But you do!"

Greg: "Yeah."

Tad: "You know there's memories of the past and you know that there's memories of the future. And so, how do you know? Do you know what I mean? I mean how do you, how does anybody know? And the way that you know is the way you've got it organized. Now, there's part of you that maintains it that way."

Greg: "You know there's an interesting thing here that, I don't mean to cut you off for a second."

Tad: "Sure."

Greg: "You know, I almost feel like before I had my accident and everything, I was just like that, and it's more, not that it's comfortable like that, like almost like going home. But this (gesturing to new Time Line) is like where the direction has come to."

Tad: "When did you have your accident? Around age 23?"

Greg: "Yeah. In '72, I had that accident..."

Tad: "Got it."

Greg: "Yeah. And I had an accident and left this little earth for a while, and the man said go back home and try it one more time. So, here I am."

Tad: "And that's probably why you're here. So why don't you float up above your Time Line again, just for fun, 'cause, hey, we wouldn't want to do anything unless it was fun, right?"

Greg: "Right on."

Tad: "So, float up above your Time Line again, and I'd like you to look back toward the past, and uh, I'd like you to notice what memories are back there that are sort of dark, or darker-colored."

Greg: "I'll tell you it (motioning to Time Line) went directly over there, but instead of coming off, like getting the vibe that it was 'whoosh' like that, it's like it went 'vroom.'"

Tad: "OK. Good."

Greg: "OK? Only real fast like it came out of the back of my head, really, you know, like a rocket blast, and shot around the corner and took off. You know it cheated on me, OK? The other one is over here and it's still over here and it's still going like this."

Tad: "OK."

Greg: "It's quit going like this, but it's going like this." (Gestures showing movement)

Tad: "Good. And, uh, it may take you, uh, a couple more minutes for you to get comfortable with it being there, you know? And you've been operating it with the other way for so long, I mean, hey, what's a couple of minutes, right?"

Greg: "Well, I'll tell you, because of my beliefs, my faith, uh, sometimes when I indulge too much information to the wrong sources, I get cut off."

Tad: "Cut off by (Pause)"

Greg: "Upstairs. OK?"

Tad: "OK."

Greg: "And so it's like I'm getting the vibes right now, from there, that I'm going to let you stabilize rather than rock your boat."

Tad: "Good."

Greg: "OK? That's the vibe I'm getting here about this."

Tad: "Right. OK."

Greg: "It's like I was playing tug of war here, for a minute, not within myself. I felt, I thought it was that and it was like playing tug of war, like two people. But now it's like, OK, now, I'm going to let you go, you know, so the rope, I got ninety percent of the rope over on my side right now, but that..."

Tad: "And I want you to continue, I want you to maintain whatever connection you need to maintain with your higher self, and notice that the connection that you need to maintain with your higher self is different from the organization of your Time Line. OK?"

Greg: "OK. Run that by me again."

Tad: "I want you to maintain whatever connection you need to maintain with your higher self. That's good."

Greg: "Whoosh. Man! OK. Keep going."

Tad: "And the Time Line is different from how you connect to your higher self. Just make sure that the Time Line is organized left to right, uh, and the connection with your higher self is, uh, different from that. Does that make sense?"

Greg: "Yeah."

Tad: "See, we're talking about an organization of memories right now, we're not talking about (Pause) because I think it's important that everyone has a connection with his higher self. OK?"

Greg: "Yeah."

Tad: "That's real important. That's very important for you to maintain. Uh..."

Greg: "I just don't want to lose what just happened. I can handle... chew gum and walk and talk at the same time." (Writes some notes.) "OK. Go ahead. I'm paying one hundred percent attention."

Tad: "All right."

Greg: "OK. He wants to see what I did here."

Tad: "You've got something good?"

Greg: "What? No. I just uh, (Pause) it just really threw me for a blast, kinda."

Tad: "Well, is this stuff heavy enough or what?"

Greg: "Well, it is to me, because, you know, a lot of my, a lot of why I'm stagnant right here is 'cause, you know..."

Tad: "And you just discovered something about that, didn't you?"

Greg: "Well, you just put me on two different planes, and I felt like I was, I went from that to this, to, to, to a cross, which is now all of a sudden, just went wham! And I mean my, you know, I'm talking like the difference between soul and physical body just went through a change."

Tad: "That's right."

Greg: "You know, and to me that's like, you know, that's kinda, kinda, kinda heavy!"

Tad: "And that's OK, isn't it?"

Greg: "You got me shaking like a little kid." (Laughs nervously)

Tad: "And I want you to discover how good it feels. I want you to discover all the good things about this, because (Pause) I think you know inside that, uh, they are real positive (Pause) don't you?"

Greg: "Oh yeah."

Tad: "And you've got some new things and you will have in the next few days to discover how, how positive these changes are going to be, and how..."

Greg: "Those are my [Time] Lines now; this is... the present."

Tad: "Great! So, what's that?"

Greg: "That is whatever the Hell just happened to me. That, I don't know, that was like a connection, almost like a break, you know, like a short circuit."

Tad: "And now it's connected again?"

Greg: "Yeah. It's connected. The only thing is that it stayed the same, and I wanted to see, when you were talking, I wanted to see what that line was, and was it going to stay the same. So, in order for me to see it in my mind again, I had to get it down on paper."

Tad: "OK. How was your Time Line originally?"

Greg: "It was up to back, and then I brought it around like that."

Tad: "And now how is it?"

Greg: "Right now it's like this (gestures), this is pretty stable right now. I still feel a tendency to want to go like that, but..."

Tad: "Well, we'll handle that in a moment."

Greg: "OK."

Tad: "That's good. though. (Pause) OK. (Some procedural discussion)

Greg: "Does that happen, I mean, is that kosher?"

Tad: "Remember, I told you earlier we were going to work with the operating system?" (Referring to the theory that many NLP techniques work on the level of the operating system of the brain, as opposed to the content or data involved with memories.)

Greg: "Uh huh. Are we talking about our quarters again, and our three boxes?"

Tad: "No, no, no. We're talking about, remember we're talking about, we're not manipulating data."

Greg: "Yeah."

Tad: "We're working on the operating system, and that's why the experience that you've had so far has been what it has been."

Greg: "Well, what I meant was, you know you were talking about a higher plane, and, and (Pause) I don't know what I was saying" (trails off)

Tad: "I want you to see that you can maintain the connection with your higher self."

Greg: "Oh yeah."

Tad: "And that your memories and memories of the future are separate from that, which you've got. That was a real good thing to do."

Greg: "Yeah, it was like…"

Tad: "Good work."

Greg: "You know, it was like when you pull a plug out of the wall at night and you see the blue spark?"

Tad: "Uh huh."

Greg: "Well if you pull it out…"

Tad: "You saw a blue spark in there?"

Greg: "Yeah. Well, it was real red. Damn near red, red, about the color of your tie."

Tad: "Good."

Greg: "You know when you pulled the plug out, if… it's almost like, you know, when you pull it out, you think, well, if I was experimenting, if I just pull it out and it sparked, I might just maintain that spark."

Tad: "Right."

Greg: "You know and, so like…"

Tad: "I got it."

Greg: "So when it came out, I thought I was going to lose it for a second, but it didn't…"

Tad: "And those sparks that happen inside, though…"

Greg: "But it stayed."

Tad: "Are maintained."

Greg: "It stayed. It got real shaky. You know, like any current, any time you, you know, two magnets—you can pull 'em so far apart they'll… anyway, it went back together."

Tad: "OK. Good. An experimental thought to share with you that you can just hear, and then think of later, is that perhaps these experiences, or these states, like the spark, are something that's always there, and what shakes is your perception. Not the spark itself. Especially on things that have truth for you. Things that have genuine truth..."

Greg: "Yeah."

Tad: "... are always there, and frequently, it almost seems as if our experience of living is one of, as if somebody or self or whatever is trying to get us to pay attention to what's happening, rather than create happening, just be really truthfully aware of what's going on."

Greg: "Oh yeah. I feel that one hundred percent. You know, like I said, the man says, 'Hey, you didn't do it right. Go back down and try it again. I'm going to give you a second shot.'"

Tad: "There's plenty of time. (Pause) Now, when you look back on your Time Line, if you were to just float up a little bit and look back at age 22 or so, is that still black or is the whole thing..."

Greg: "Well."

Tad: "Lightened up and evened up and become an experience which you..."

Greg: "That age, you know, my daughter was born with all kinds of problems, you know, but life was good, so it, it's like, you know, when you look at a light bulb and then you look away you see things but you still, once the brightness is gone you still see the spot a little bit, you know..."

Tad: "OK."

Greg: "That's the way it is. It would be like a gray."

Tad: "So, the area that was dark has sort of lightened up since we (Laughter) **made that change**."

Greg: "Yeah."

Tad: "Good."

Greg: "There's like a void in there. You know, you asked me about voids. That's where the void is—I have a memory loss at that time. You know, from being in the hospital, and I went twenty-one days in a coma and I don't remember 'Jack Didley.'"

Tad: "Yeah."

Greg: "So, uh, there's a memory loss in there."

Tad: "Now, when you go back and think about that time, if you could, do it now for example, do you, um, come up with a lot of emotion or a lot of feelings on that or is it pretty well flat for you at this point?"

Greg: "Well, it's been long enough and I've dealt with it long enough that it's, uh..."

Tad: "Is there trauma there, though, is there, like do you get nervous or upset when you think of it?"

Greg: "No. (Pause) You know when they say, like, oh, we're going to hypnotize you and take you back through this thing to blah, blah, blah, it's almost like that. In order for me, you know, because I can't remember. No matter what I've done to try to remember, or people have tried to do, you know, it's like (Pause) the only way you're going to get it, man, is if I hypnotize you and make you come through it, type thing, you know like on a spook movie, type thing..."

Tad: "Sure. Sure."

Greg: "Because I don't see any other way, you know, and I've thought about it, because there was an accident that took place, it was partially my fault and mostly the other guy's fault, and, uh, being as I don't even remember being there, you know, I had to have people bring me up to date from wherever I was in, like, up to the time of the accident. I remember my day at work."

Tad: "OK."

Greg: "And I remember an incident just before quitting time but from that time on, I can't tell you a damn thing."

Tad: "Is there any value to go back and recover that at this point, or do we just let that go?"

Greg: "You know, I can't tell you a damn' thing, and then about within, say, 45 minutes to an hour from that time I got off work, and now I'm telling you what I've been told, you know, where I've come up to, and I had an accident. OK?"

Tad: "And I'm wondering what effect that has on the presenting problem." (Procedural discussion about going back to an earlier problem than the one just mentioned.) "What I want you to do now is to float up above your Time Line."

Greg: "Above my Time Line?"

Tad: "Again. Float up above your Time Line, again."

Greg: "OK. That takes a second."

Tad: "And I want you to go back, uh, to a much younger time, somewhere between the ages of zero and seven, and, uh…"

Greg: "OK. Go for it."

Tad: "And around age, uh, (Pause) well, just float back in there and see if there are any dark areas in those areas, in those years."

Greg: "Yeah. Oh, yeah."

Tad: "OK. That's what I thought. So, uh, what's the earliest dark area? Around age, uh…"

Greg: "Oh, about one-zero, or zero-one, let's put it that way."

Tad: "OK. How about between ages, uh…"

Greg: "Not one-zero. Zero-one, I told you."

Tad: "Yeah. Yeah. Yeah. All right. Between zero and one, huh?"

Greg: "No. I mean like…"

Tad: "Before you were born?"

Greg: "To date, yeah. You got it."

Tad: "Before you were born. OK. Before you were born. So there's something that's going on in the womb?"

Greg: "No. This is prior."

Tad: "Oh. Prior to that. OK. Good. (Pause) Now, uh, so float up above your Time Line."

Greg: "I'm up there, man."

Tad: "I want you to get way up there. And I want you to look at the pr... Now, are you talking about this particular occurrence that happened..."

Greg: "Do you want pre-existence?"

Tad: "I want to know if it happened during a previous lifetime, or did it..."

Greg: "OK. Let me rap, and maybe that will help answer and then we can go from there, OK?"

Tad: "Sure."

Greg: "Uh. (Pause) OK. I'm in, from my terms, we can decipher that in a minute, I'm in a celestial state, OK? A spiritual state."

Tad: "You're in there, this is before you were born."

Greg: "This is as a spirit. OK?"

Tad: "Uh huh."

Greg: "And, uh, I have a choice to make, right? And that's who's going to be my Mom and Dad, and all that..."

Tad: "Right."

Greg: "Stuff. OK. I made a decision, you know? (Long pause) God damn! Excuse me."

Tad: "And? (Pause) So this is pre-existence?"

Greg: (Pause) "You know, this thing is so easy. He's f—-ing with my head so easy." (Laughs)

Tad: "And it's good, isn't it?"

Greg: "I know this in me, and I've rapped with people about it, OK. And I've explained things to certain people that I've felt could relate, and you know, uh, I don't know what your beliefs are or anything like that, and I wouldn't do that unless I got to know you, you know, buddies, and we went out running around, whatever, reading *Playboy*, and whatever it is, you know, I mean so that there's some co-relation, you know. I can take it so far, and I'm going to drop it."

Tad: "And did you see Vanna White in the latest issue, that's what I want to know!!!"

Greg: (Laughter) "But I mean, anyway, long story short, back to where we're at, uh, I had a choice. Now I bullshitted too much, and" (Trails off)

Tad: "Now that's all right. You said you had a choice, now, here's what I want to know. Was it in a previous lifetime or was it in the space between lifetimes?"

Greg: "Previous lifetime. So, now I have this choice to make, and the given, to me, is not real clear on the one hand, because I didn't make that choice, so it's not about nothing. What's relevant is the choice I made, which is: If you go down this road, if you go down there and you take that, you know, in other words, I'm going to be with this family, this is going to be my sister and all this, this is what you have to take with you. And what I took with me was, OK, you know, I'm going to face, uh, uh, that's what I accept for life—in other words, my lot in life, OK. You know, I'm gonna have eight brothers and sisters to contend with. Going to have a mother, uh, I don't get along with, uh, you know, uh, that kind of stuff, you know, um. Also going to take on another problem which you might be driving at which is (and I'm going to go back up here for a second, but) is that, (Pause) (hard to do three things at once) is that, I was going to take on the exception of, you know, hey, I'm going to come as a crippled person or a, you know, I'm going to have some kind of physical, mental, whatever, and I chose that mental, OK? And the mental thing was that I was going to be dyslexic or whatever we want to call it for now. OK?"

Tad: "Uh huh."

Greg: "OK. Give me a second before you shoot any questions at me." (Pause)

Tad: "It's all right."

Greg: "OK."

Tad: "You ready?"

Greg: (Whispers) "Yeah."

Tad: "I want you to float right out to now."

Greg: "Oh, shit. Here I spent all this time getting back. OK."

Tad: "That's right. Float right out to now. We're going to take you back there in a minute, but I want you to float right out to now. And I want you to look out in the future."

Greg: "...I'm over here."

Tad: "I want you to float out in the future."

Greg: "OK. I'm there."

Tad: "And I want you to look back toward now."

Greg: "OK."

Tad: "And what I want you to notice is (Pause) uh, or let me ask you a question. I guess I can ask you a question, rather than... because I would rather it come from you, I want you to notice if all these things that you came here for today are gone, because the question is, you've suffered enough, now is it OK to let go of them? See when you go out into the future and look back toward now..."

Greg: "OK. You're asking me for a yes-or-no answer, and I can't guarantee that one."

Tad: "So, all I want you to get is that when you go out into the future and look back toward now, I want you to notice what you've got, what you came down here with, perhaps, and I just want to put forth a possibility, that perhaps you paid your dues."

Greg: "Yeah. I'm just... I'll go for that."

Tad: "Can you buy that theory?"

Greg: "Yeah."

Tad: "Perhaps you've paid your dues, and that's why you're here (gesturing to the seat he's in), and while you had some affliction or something to make up for or something to do, or you had to take a certain choice, or have this certain..."

Greg: "Uh huh."

Tad: "But now it's OK for you to **be OK**."

Greg: "I'll buy that."

Tad: "So, what I want you to do is to go out into the future and look back toward now and notice that all this stuff here is OK".

Greg: "I'll buy that. It feels shaky. But I'll, yeah, I'll go along with that."

Tad: "It may be shaky, but I want you to notice that as you look back toward now, that **it's OK**."

Greg: "OK. I want to interject something before I forget about it."

Tad: "OK. Sure."

Greg: "You know, when you asked me about, about knowing about this, my sister threw this on me about, you know, closing my eyes and going 'chew,' 'chew.' Right? She threw that at me. OK. She didn't say nothing to me about it, what was what. She just said, 'I want you to close your eyes,' you know. And what was it, 'Put your hand…'"

(Discussion about Time Line work previously done with sister, who had previously come in for therapy with author.)

Greg: "… and I had a void. You know that void I told you I had right there? Well, I don't feel that void any more."

Tad: "**That's right**. That's 'cause we made the connections."

Greg: "Yeah. OK."

Tad: "That's what happened when we made those connections earlier."

Greg: "See, 'cause I told her I start here…" (More discussion about Time Line work previously done with sister.)

Tad: "That **was**, was the way it was, but now it is the way it is. Like it? Good. Let's go back in the past again. Let's go out to the past and go back into the, uh, time when you were making choices."

Greg: "Back up."

Tad: "Yeah. Float up above your Time Line again, (Pause) go back into the past, and this is the time, uh…"

Greg: "Bob Dylan, 'Knock, Knock, Knockin' on Heaven's Door,' OK, I'm ready."

Tad: "OK."

Greg: "He says, 'Quit ignoring me, get it on.' OK. Let's go, I'm ready."

Tad: "So, I want you to go back into the, into the past, there."

Greg: "OK."

Tad: "Uh, before your birth."

Greg: "All right."

Tad: "And, uh, look at yourself having made that decision, OK?"

Greg: "Yeah. Go ahead. Keep running it."

Tad: "Uh, I want you to notice that you have some feelings about that decision."

Greg: "What we discussed was, was that cleared up and everything? That decision is OK. In other words, I'm done beating Greg————- with a stick."

Tad: "And you're OK with the decision now."

Greg: "But now we step from that block to another block which is, you know…"

Tad: "What is that block?"

Greg: "… taking the step into my mom's womb."

Tad: "I just want to make sure where we are 'cause I want to be real clear about it."

Greg: "Yeah. That's why I brought you here."

Tad: "You're OK with the stuff previous to your birth?"

Greg: "Yeah."

Tad: "OK. Let's go look at what's going on in your mom's womb now."

Greg: "OK."

Tad: "So, uh…"

Greg: "What is it?"

Tad: "Yeah, you got any, is there some trauma there, or what?"

Greg: "Yeah, there's still a, ah, you know, uh, that, have you ever heard the saying that, the Lord says I'll take you hot or cold but not lukewarm?"

Tad: "Uh huh. So, which are you?"

Greg: "The reason for my little thing is for being lukewarm. And now, I'm wanting to be lukewarm, only knowing I've got to make a choice that I've already made. It's like I want to back out of it."

Tad: "So it's like you're in your mom's womb and you want to back out of that decision?"

Greg: "And so my mom went through a real long labor (I'll make this short but get enough out), and when I was born they had to use whatever they call forceps or something. But I constantly, instead of, when a child's born, they come out, I wanted to stay in. I did anything and everything to get back up."

Tad: "So, I want you to know that was something you did then."

Greg: "OK. So, anyway, then I was born and here I am."

Tad: "Now."

Greg: "But that's always given me a trauma thing."

Tad: "So since you've gone through that right now…"

Greg: "And, but I want to interject this, because there's some reason for this. Uh, because I'm OK, me personally, but there's still a hangup… My mother almost died and, but I feel a real darkness, you know, it's her darkness, not mine…"

Tad: "So, you know it's hers?"

Greg: "... Yeah, it's her darkness, and either I die or live at her expense, so it's up to me to make that choice..."

Tad: "So you did make that choice."

Greg: "Yeah, and my mother and I have always had a, you know, we don't like... I don't like her as a person... there's still the bond of a mother and her son, and a hell of a darkness. It's like a total darkness... It's like when you look at the moon and you see the whole moon, but all there is, is the crest, and a little white line around the whole ball of the moon."

Tad: "So, it's like an eclipse."

Greg: "Yeah..."

Tad: "Well, let me just ask you a question..."

Greg: "OK."

Tad: "Could we just play for a minute and see if you can take what's eclipsing that **out of there** so that you can see the light of the moon?"

Greg: "Well, I can do it like a card, but it doesn't tell me what the problem is."

Tad: "I want you to take it out and I want you to know (Pause), you just did it?"

Greg: "Yeah."

Tad: "You don't know what the problem is, but is it OK when you've done that?"

Greg: "Yeah but I know it's a f..."(trails off). Yeah. OK. Go ahead, let's keep moving, maybe it'll take care of itself."

Tad: "Yeah. So, what's your evaluation on that? You said, 'But you know.' What do you know?"

Greg: "Well, I know I can take care of it just by pulling the card, you know, I mean like, a little slide thing..."

Tad: "OK."

Greg: "OK. Now I got a full moon, OK, great."

Tad: "Now, is that OK?"

Greg: "Yeah, it's OK. But I still feel like a..."

Tad: "Well you can keep the moon full for a moment, and I want to ask you a question. What is it that causes you to feel the need, or what is it that used to cause you to feel the need to have to keep that dark, and what is it that could make you be OK with having it be OK, now?"

Greg: (Pause) "Uh, I'm OK now."

Tad: "I know."

Greg: "It just took care of itself."

Tad: "Good job."

(Discussion about event that disappeared.)

Tad: "Just let it go. It's not yours either."

(More discussion about event.)

Tad: "OK. Let's work on that now. Now, let's just say that your mom had all this trauma with your birth, and that, uh, she was, that's the way she was, I mean, she was traumatized, she almost died, and so unconsciously, perhaps, she blamed you. Uh. So, again when you look at..."

Greg: "Yeah. Unconsciously, she blamed, she blamed me!!! OK!"

Tad: "Yeah. Now, but I want you to know, and you know now, just as of this minute, or just a couple of minutes ago, that it's not your fault."

Greg: "Yeah."

Tad: "It's nothing to do with you."

Greg: "Yeah. I know that. I've always known that. But you're right she, she, I mean those are the vibes I'm getting from California. She did!!"

Tad: "Now, what I want you to do is to look back and notice that her contract, you talk about your contract, her contract with life..."

Greg: "OK."

Tad: "... her contract was to almost die in childbirth."

Greg: "OK. I can handle that."

Tad: "OK. You got that?"

Greg: "Yeah. That helps keep the window clean."

Tad: "So what I want you to know is that you're not responsible for her contract."

Greg: "Yeah. I got that."

Tad: "All right, and she, however she is, is however she is. Now, and that doesn't diminish you as a person, it's just her contract. That's her stuff. That's the stuff that she needs to handle from her past, but it has nothing to do with you."

(Discussion about the event.)

Tad: "And therefore are you then healed at this point about this event?"

Greg: "I'm OK, Doc..."

Tad: "I can tell that."

(More discussion about the event.)

Tad: "Now, what I want you to do is I want you to notice in your past that just going back and cleaning up that stuff cleaned up a lot of other stuff in your past..."

Greg: "Yeah."

Tad: "And I can already see that in your face."

Greg: "Yeah. Oh, yeah. I can feel the difference."

Tad: "Look at how much different he is. Really major shift. Now, what I want to do is, I want to ask you about your self-worth, because see, I want you to notice that your self-worth, your image of your self-esteem has changed."

Greg: "Yeah."

Tad: "See, 'cause it, now I want you to go back in the past. Just float up above your Time Line again and go back in the past, and

I want you to see if there's any other pockets there of negativity that came from your mom, or any other stuff we need to clean up, or can your unconscious, has it already made those connections that it needed to make to..."

Greg: "No. There are still a few dark spots in there dealing with the dyslexic stuff. My mom's, you know, negative, constant negative drive, you know."

Tad: "We haven't cleaned up the dyslexia yet, so that's OK, leave that there, but I..."

Greg: "That's why I mentioned it right now."

Tad: "We're gonna. We're making real good progress. We'll get to it, but I want to, I just want to make sure that, uh, that we've got a lot of the stuff with your mom cleaned up."

Greg: "Pretty much. Maybe I need to go back upstairs and find out what I'm bringing in, but we're up to about [age] 6 or 7 and then we're going to hit the dyslexic stuff, so I need to go back up to tell you about where you can come in at, and take it from there."

Tad: "All right, tell me."

Greg: (Pause) "There's a hell of a rejection period from about, (Pause) well that's pretty clear, I can clear that..."

Tad: "Notice how these things **just begin to clear up** once you learn the process..."

Greg: "You know, yeah. And you deal with it real quick, and just 'cause, I just flashed the card right by real quick..."

Tad: "That's right."

Greg: "... and I don't care how fast they go as long as I see it. Uh. Yeah. We'll stick with it. (Pause) From about thirteen until I left home, which was pretty young, well it was fifteen, uh, I don't want to blame that on momma, 'cause that's her hang-up, not mine, hang in there man..." (Laughter)

Tad: "You're going to make all these changes and you won't leave anything for me to do (Laughter), which is the kind of work I like to do, you know."

Greg: "Yeah." (Laughter) "Kick back and get paid for it... (Laughter) Uh, let's see. Well, just to kind of fill you in real quick on the gaps, is what it is, is that I've gone through in that thirteen-to-fifteen-year-old age, a real lot of harassment in school. I was a real rowdy kid..."

Tad: "Hey. Wouldn't you be if somebody gave you all that shit and told you, you couldn't, uh..."

Greg: "Yeah. And I had a lot of anxieties because there were things I wanted to do, I wanted to be a Forest Ranger that worked in the towers, you know?"

Tad: "Uh huh."

Greg: "... and spot forest fires... (Describes decision not to do this) ... and I just went through that plane, and washed that and went through the next stage which was my marriage (Describes mother and marriage) ... that's the hogwash I was washing out, OK."

Tad: "Looks like you're growing up."

Greg: "But there's definite, a definite darkness about, now we're into my marriage, OK. (Pause) Uh, I, when I got married, there's a three-way collision here. You know, my wife, me and my mother, 'cause my mother, this is back to like I was saying about your babies, is my mother, uh it's damn near like she wanted to be your friend, and your mother, your lover, your everything, you know?"

Tad: "Yeah."

Greg: "And I couldn't accept all that."

Tad: "Some people don't know when to **let go**."

Greg: "Yeah. And so, my mother (Describes more about relationship with mother).

Tad: "Now that's real important."

Greg: "... all my women have come back and they haven't been able to do it. And I just recently have been able to figure it out."

Tad: "So that's your mom's stuff, isn't it?"

Greg: "Yeah. This is back to my mom's stuff. Because it affects, (Pause) this isn't me, but it's the effect it has on my relationship with other women."

Tad: "So, let's talk for a minute about your mom and the women, and what I want you to look at is, I want you to look at how you can let your mom let you go, inside yourself, for you to let go."

Greg: "Oh. (Pause) That's taken care of already. I've done that part right there, as far as that relationship. (Pause) I can't bring my mother back into my life in any sort of way..."

Tad: "Not yet. And there's no need to until **you're ready**."

Greg: "Yeah."

Tad: "And I want you to know that I don't get that **you're ready right now**."

Greg: "No."

Tad: "Be sure you're ready before you do... Now, here's a notion about things, what you perceive is what you believe. And what is in your world, because millions of literally millions of pieces of information are in our world, and we only perceive a few hundred of them clumped into about seven chunks, so we're deleting about virtually everything, we're generalizing about virtually everything and we're distorting about everything. It's being filtered through those beliefs and values that we created early on in life. And that's our experience. So if you're deleting everything, no one can do anything to you that you're not doing to yourself, and therefore frequently, this is good news, 'cause the shorthand here is, if there's a real asshole in your life, the way to change that asshole and heal that asshole is to change and heal yourself, and that asshole will suddenly become an angel, and you'll wonder why, but you'll go, 'Hey, who cares, just **do it now**.' And then you go, 'Oh yeah.' So frequently the stuff you were telling me, to get conscious about it for a moment, you were telling me about mom and how you didn't want to get born, and how you made a decision that you later regretted, and how you fought tooth and nail not to come out, and she's sitting there going, 'Jeez, this is putting me on the brink here, physically.' So, in a way if you want to look at who started it, who did start it?"

Greg: "I did. So that's why I put the guilt trip, and accepted the guilt trip, when it was laid back..."

Tad: "And if she didn't need that, if that wasn't appropriate for her, it wouldn't have been in her life either."

Greg: "It takes two to tango."

Tad: "But you can heal your own by forgiving yourself, seeing what you did with, oh, you made some decision, great. Make some new ones. It's never too late. That's important, let's talk about decisions... the word decision in language... is a 'nominalization;' it's a process word turned into a noun. Problem with that is that when you turn it into a noun it seems so final. A decision. But actually what decision is, is the **process of deciding**. See, you decided to be here. You're still here."

Greg: "Yeah."

Tad: "That was why some of the things, maybe you were taking drugs, but guess what? It didn't work? 'Cause you're still here. That's the bitch of it, but the beauty of that is you are still here and now you can begin to make choices and move forward, or move off that way (points to future). Deciding is just the process of deciphering, so deciding is just seeing what you see. So it's really perceiving, and now you have the chance to perceive it anew and perceive it from different angles..."

(Discussion about communication and Greg's ability to communicate.)

Tad: "OK. Now. So, what I want you to do is to look at your marriage and make sure **that's OK**, because your unconscious mind is very quick."

Greg: "Well, it's over now, but I mean..."

Tad: "But I want you to look, float up above your Time Line again and look from ages zero up through 22."

Greg: "OK. Where my marriage was."

Tad: "And I want you to notice that a lot of that stuff in the past that used to give you, uh, bothersomeness, that used to, say, bother you in the past has now been cleaned up, and as you look at it (Pause) that a lot of the shifts that we've made have generalized to other areas in the past that **were** a problem but have now been cleared up."

Greg: "Hold off a minute, let me go back and sweep my closet." (Pause)

Tad: "All right." (Pause)

Greg: "You know, it's amazing how fast you can clean one out and there's nothing in it."

Tad: (Laughs) "Wouldn't it be interesting if it was this easy to change?"

Greg: "OK. I'm happy with Greg up until we're married. OK. Go on. On with the show."

Tad: (Laughs) "OK. Those things which you have just done you can continue off into the future."

Greg: "What, sweep it?"

Tad: "Yeah."

Greg: "Yeah, but it's like sweeping over a bump and pushing a ball out of the way."

Tad: "Straighten it out."

Greg: "And the problem is, rather than going out the door, 'whoosh,' with the dust, 'cause we don't care about the dust, but we stop and look at the broken skate and stuff like that, so, OK, now, so they're outside the door. Still got a pile of junk to dump."

Tad: "Well, uh…"

Greg: "Dump it." (Laughter)

Tad: "No, just leave it here." (Points to a part of the office.) "That's what we do."

Greg: "That's what I'm doing. I'm leaving it on you, you got it. Naw. OK. (Pause) So, I got through the next one, I'm in another closet, let's get on."

Tad: "Notice how you can, yeah. And look at his physiology change as he does that. Just keep going right on through and clean it right up to now."

Greg: "Well, I'm at a stumbling block right now."

Tad: "OK. What do you have?"

Greg: "... I still love my wife, you know, my ex-wife. And I love my kids very much. I haven't put out much time with my kids, mostly because of the vibes between my relationship with her mother. OK. I have just recently. (Pause) OK. Closet swept. On with the next show."

Tad: "I want to talk about that for a minute. Open your eyes for a second. Um. Let's talk for a second about guilt. Because guilt is one of the, as far as I am concerned, one of the worst emotions on the planet. Nobody needs to be guilty."

Greg: "I agree with that."

Tad: "You know. I mean the stuff you did in the past, hey, you know, you want to do something about your kids in the future, you want to do something about your ex-wife in the future, that's in the future."

Greg: "Yeah."

Tad: "But whatever you've done, you've done."

Greg: "Yeah. I've cleared that up. I've taken care of that."

Tad: "OK. Uh, do you have any events in the past about which you're guilty, at the moment?"

Greg: "No, I'm clean. Like I said, I swept the closet. I just went through all the closets. We got a clean house up to now."

Tad: "OK. Look at his physiology. A major change."

Greg: "Yeah. We're upstairs, let's get to the attic, and go home."

Tad: "OK. So, I want to talk to you for a moment about dyslexia, because dyslexia is a strategy." (Knock on door. Office staff brings in a copy of *Playboy*.) "It's funny that it would have arrived just like that, isn't it?" (Laughter)

Greg: "Yeah."

Tad: "Uh. This is the June issue."

Greg: "There are no accidents."

Tad: "So, um, dyslexia is a strategy, which means it is a combination of internal processing, internal things that you do in a certain order. OK. That is to say that a lot of people who are dyslexic, uh, well, **can you read the cover**?" (Pause) "I mean the words!" (Laughter)

Greg: "I thought you meant the knit and the lace."

(Discussion about the cover of the magazine and therapy on dyslexia. Therapy on dyslexia has been omitted from this transcript.)

(Hands the magazine to Greg.)

Tad: "Here it is."

Greg: "Yeah. Read it and tell me what's on page 92." (Laughs)

Tad: "OK. I just want to check one more thing... your Time Line is like that?" (Gestures left to right.)

Greg: "Yeah."

Tad: "So, under what kind of circumstance can you imagine it possible to be compelled to do coke? Can you think of a circumstance, is the compulsion there?"

Greg: "No. There's no compulsion. In fact the only time I've ever really had an urge and gone off is when I've been freaking out with a bunch of chicks. (Pause) And right now, I feel like I'm saying, 'Ah, that's cool, you guys go off and have a good time, 'cause I'm doing my thing'."

Tad: "So that's the only situation that you think you'd be compelled, at that point, or..." (Pause)

Greg: "Yeah. That's what comes to my mind, the only time that I could think that might even make me take a second look at it."

Tad: "So as you imagine that..."

Greg: "'Cause I'm a freak."

Tad: "So as you imagine that, what I'd like you to do is I'd like you to **compartmentalize that** particular thing. And what I'd like you to do is to **separate the issue of sex** which is really **appropriate** with large numbers, of..." (Laughter)

Greg: "Now, let's be generous here."

Tad: "Now, what I want you to do is I want you to make a picture of how you would..." (Pause) "Can you get back that compulsion?"

Greg: "It's like I have a twinge, but it's like it's cool."

Tad: "There's **no compulsion** there?"

Greg: (Surprised) "No. There isn't. It's like a, it's a, 'no.' What I'm saying is it's a 'no' from me 'cause I'm not feeling that much of a desire to make that much of a sacrifice, because of what I know of its cost."

Tad: "Good. So that's one thing... I wanted to check one more thing. Have you ever been in a situation where you did something and then you said you'd never do it? So, you quit and then you went back. You quit and then you went back? And finally you said, 'This is it, this is the last straw, I'll never do it again?'"

Greg: "Yeah. There's been a few of those. And that's one of them."

Tad: "Which one? Cocaine is?"

Greg: "Yeah."

Tad: "But you, but... OK. Something other than cocaine, where you said you'd never go back and do it again."

Greg: "Uh. Yeah. There's been things, you know, uh, made the mistake, told the old lady some white lie about something and, uh, never done it again."

Tad: "How about something heavier than that? Any behavior that you said, you did, and then you didn't want to do, then went back and did it again, and then finally you said, **'That's it, I quit, and I'm done with it.'** There was a last straw. What was that?"

(Discussion about that event and elicitation of the "last straw pattern developed by Richard Bandler. For a complete description of the pattern, see *Change Your Mind and Keep The Change,* Steve Andreas, 1987.)

Tad: "And then the words that you're saying in your mind at the same time is that the next time, you're going to be dead, there isn't going to be any next time, something like that?"

Greg: "Yeah. Basically that's what I'm saying right then, and then, 'Hey asshole, are you going to sit there and watch yourself do this? Is it worth all these reruns or do you think that, you know, the next one you ain't going to be able to see the rerun?' So I chose that there ain't going to be no rerun."

Tad: "OK. Good. Now, I want you to think about your most recent decision to stop doing coke."

Greg: "OK that's a few minutes ago."

Tad: "You said you've been off it for a while."

Greg: "Oh. OK. (Pause) Well, my recent decision, well whatever, OK, let's go on."

Tad: "Or did you just recently just decide to stop doing it, like recently?"

Greg: "Well when I said right now, I meant present, yeah, because then I had decided to, but now I've got a conviction. It's like you can say, 'I'm not walking across the street no more,' but then your hat blows across the street and you go across the street, but now it's 'Oh, so there goes my hat, so it costs a hundred bucks, big deal.'"

Tad: "So make a picture of yourself having quit, done doing coke."

Greg: "Yeah, I got it."

Tad: "I want you to make it similar to the picture that when you sat down with your girlfriend the second time." (Pause)

Greg: "OK."

Tad: "And I want to ask you a question."

Greg: "OK."

Tad: "Are you ready? (Pause) Hey asshole, are you going to watch yourself do it again, 'cause the next one you're going to be dead."

Greg: (Laughs) "Yeah. I got it. I got it."

Tad: "You know what I'm saying. There's not going to be a next time."

Greg: "Right. I got it."

Tad: "Now, you got that inside?"

Greg: "Yeah. I had that already."

Tad: "You already did that one with the coke?"

Greg: "I did that while we were going through it."

Tad: "Good job."

Greg: "... I already made that decision."

Tad: "Got it. OK. Now, I want you to think of a time in the future when you might be like thinking you might be with some women, more than one." (Laughs)

Greg: "Naw, one's cool."

Tad: "One's cool. And, uh..."

Greg: "One's more than sufficient. Three's a handful." (Laughter and joking)

Tad: "When you think of that, is it possible to get any of those old twinges of doing it or is **it gone**?"

Greg: "No. It's gone. Before we were talking about it, yeah, I could feel it lighten up. But no, it's not there now."

Tad: "Try it."

Greg: "I don't have to look at it. I can see it without closing my eyes. Yeah. I can picture without closing. It's gone."

Tad: "Good. Uh, OK... I think that's it. And all the processes we've done are interesting processes that you can continue to do on your own. Either consciously or unconsciously."

(Additional discussion and cleanup)

Tad: "So here's a copy of **Playboy**. Go read it, quickly."

In two follow-up interviews, client told us that he not only has remained free from further drug use, but also reads *Playboy*'s jokes in fifteen minutes. The client remains free from cocaine use six months after therapy.

Bibliography

Andreas, Steve; Andreas, Connirae. *Change Your Mind—And Keep The Change*. Real People Press, Moab, Utah, 1987.

Bandler, Leslie Cameron; et al. *Know How*. FuturePace, Inc., San Rafael, California, 1985.

Bandler, Leslie Cameron. *Solutions*. FuturePace, Inc., San Rafael, California, 1985.

———. *The Emotional Hostage*. Futurepace, Inc., San Rafael, California, 1986.

———. *The Emprint Method*. FuturePace, Inc., San Rafael, California, 1985.

Bandler, Richard. *Magic In Action*. Meta Publications, Cupertino, California, 1984.

———. *Using Your Brain—For A Change*. Real People Press, Moab, Utah, 1985.

Bandler, Richard; Grinder, John. *Frogs Into Princes*. Real People Press, Moab, Utah, 1979.

———. *Patterns Of The Hypnotic Techniques Of Milton H. Erickson, M.D.* Meta Publications, Cupertino, California, 1975.

———. *Reframing*. Real People Press, Moab, Utah, 1982.

———. *The Structure Of Magic I*. Science and Behavior Books, Palo Alto, California, 1975.

———. *The Structure Of Magic II*. Science and Behavior Books, Palo Alto, California, 1976.

————. *Trance-Formations*. Real People Press, Moab, Utah, 1981.

Bandler, Richard; Grinder, John; Delozier, Judith. *Patterns Of The Hypnotic Techniques Of Milton H. Erickson, M.D., Volume 2*. Meta Publications, Cupertino, California, 1977.

Braid, James, M.R.C.S.E., C.M.W.S.&c. *Neurypnology*. John Churchill, Edinburgh, Scotland, 1843.

de Bono, Edward. *Lateral Thinking*. Harper & Row, Publishers, New York, New York, 1973.

Dilts, Robert; et al. *Neuro Linguistic Programming: Volume I*. Meta Publications, Cupertino, California, 1980.

Erickson, Milton H., M.D. *Life Reframing In Hypnosis*. Irvington Publishers Inc., New York, New York, 1985.

Erickson, Milton H., M.D.; Cooper, Linn F. *Time Distortion In Hypnosis*. Irvington Publishers, Inc., New York, New York, 1982.

Erickson, Milton H., M.D.; Hershman, Seymour, M.D.; Secter, Irving I., D.D.S. *The Practical Application of Medical and Dental Hypnosis*. The Julian Press, Inc., New York, New York, 1961.

Erickson, Milton H.; Rossi, Ernest. *Experiencing Hypnosis*. Irvington Publishers, New York, New York, 1981.

————. *Hypnotic Realities*. Irvington Publishers, New York, New York, 1976.

————. *Hypnotherapy*. Irvington Publishers, New York, New York, 1979.

Hall, Edward T. *Beyond Culture*. Doubleday & Company, Inc., Garden City, New York, 1976.

————. *The Dance of Life*. Doubleday & Company, Inc., Garden City, New York, 1984.

————. *The Hidden Dimension*. Doubleday & Company, Inc., Garden City, New York, 1969.

————. *The Silent Language*. Doubleday & Company, Inc., Garden City, New York, 1973.

Jaynes, Julian. *The Origin Of Consciousness In The Breakdown Of The Bicameral Mind*. Houghton Mifflin Company, Boston, Massachusetts, 1976.

Jung, C. G. *Psychological Types*. Princeton University Press, Princeton, New Jersey, 1971.

Keirsey, David; Bates, Marilyn. *Please Understand Me*. Gnosology Books Ltd., Del Mar, California, 1984.

Korzybsk, Alfred. *Science and Sanity*. The International Non-Aristotelian Library Publishing Company, Lakeville, Connecticut, 1933.

Lewis, Byron A.; Puclik, R. Frank. *Magic Demystified*. Metamorphous Press, Lake Oswego, Oregon, 1982.

Rossi, Ernest Lawrence. *The Psychobiology of Mind Body Healing*. W. W. Norton & Co., New York, New York, 1986.

Wetterstrand, O. *Hypnotism and Its Application to Practical Medicine*. New York, New York, 1902.

Glossary

Adaptive—The Myers-Briggs Judger-Perceiver Category.

Adler—One of the fathers of modern Psychology along with Freud, and Jung.

Affiliating—The need of human beings to affiliate with each other. One of the complex Meta Programs which indicates whether a person will prefer to work alone or with a team.

Align—Arrange so that all the elements being aligned are parallel, and therefore moving in the same direction.

Ambiguity—The use of language which is vague, or ambiguous, Language which is ambiguous is also abstract (as opposed to specific).

Analogue—Having shades of meaning, as opposed to Digital which has discrete (on or off) meaning. As in an analogue watch (a watch with minute and hour hands).

Anchor—A specific stimulus which, when applied, produces a specific response. The application may be, as in NLP, purposeful.

Anglo-European—In this context, refers to a certain way of experiencing time as proposed by Edward T. Hall, and is closest to Through Time.

Anxiety—A non-specific apprehension about the future.

Association—As in a memory, for example, looking through your own eyes, hearing what you heard, and feeling the feelings as if you were actually there.

Attitude—A collection of Values and Beliefs around a certain subject.

Away From—When a person's preference is to move in an opposite direction from what they do not want.

Belief—A generalization about the state of the world, or our ability to act in the world. Usually organized around a Value.

Calibrate—The ability to notice changes, which occur from moment to moment in another person, using your sensory acuity.

Chunk—Noun: A group or collection of bits of information. e.g., a phone number may be either 7 chunks (as 123-4567), or 5 chunks (the exchange 123 as one chunk and the numbers 4567 as individual numbers), or two chunks (the exchange 123 as one chunk and the numbers 4567 as the other chunk). Verb: The ability to move through levels of ambiguity to specificity. (See Hierarchy of Ideas.)

Closure—The completion of a chunk of information.

Cognitive Psychology—The study of how man perceives his world.

Compulsion—As in an undeniable motivation to act in a certain way.

Convincer—One of the Meta Programs. See Convincer Strategy.

Counterfactual—Information which runs counter to fact.

Criteria—As used here, a Value.

Decision—Having completed the process of deciding, which usually (sometimes wrongly) fixes the process in time.

Deletion—One of the universal processes by which we model other human beings as when we selectively pay attention to certain aspects of our experience and not to others.

Digital—Having a discrete (on or off) meaning, as opposed to Analogue which has shades of meaning. As in a digital watch (a watch displaying numerals instead of hands).

Dissociation—As in a memory, for example, looking at your body in the picture so that you do not have the feelings you would have if you were actually there.

Distortion—One of the universal processes by which we model other human beings as when we make shifts in our experience of sensory data by making misrepresentations of data.

Down-time—As in having all sensory input channels turned inward so that there are no chunks of attention available for outward attention.

Ecology—The study of the effects of individual actions on the larger system. In an individual, the study of the effects of individual components of therapy on the bigger picture of the whole individual.

Elicitation—The act of discovery and detection of certain internal processes.

Emotion—An internal feeling.

Extravert—An attitude in the Myers-Briggs category, External Behavior, Introvert/Extravert.

Feeler—A preference in the Myers-Briggs category, Internal Process – Thinker/Feeler.

Feeling—An internal kinesthetic (evaluative kinesthetic response) or an external kinesthetic (feeling an external touch).

Generalization—One of the universal processes by which we model other human beings.

Gestalt—A collection of memories, where the memories are linked together or grouped together around a certain subject.

Guilt—An emotion (internal kinesthetic response) resulting from an experience in the past where the person experiencing guilt is ashamed about something not done.

Hierarchy—An organization of things or ideas where the more important ideas are given a ranking based upon their importance.

In Time—The organization of memories in a person where a portion of the past or present or future are either inside or behind the person.

Through Time—The organization of memories in a person where all of the past or present or future is in front of the person.

Introvert—An attitude in the Myers-Briggs category, External Behavior, Introvert/Extravert.

Intuitor—A preference in the Myers-Briggs category, Internal State, Sensor/Intuitor

Kinesthetic—An internal evaluative emotion, or an external or internal sensation.

Linguistic—Relating to language.

Matcher—Someone who compares the input data with data already known in the process of understanding something. The Matcher, in the process of understanding, will compare the similarities.

Meta Programs—One of the deepest filters to perception which is essentially a content-free filter.

Metaphor—A story. In this context a metaphor usually has the purpose of creating change in an individual.

Mismatcher—Someone who compares the input data with data already known in the process of understanding something. The Mismatcher in the process of understanding will compare the differences.

Modal Operator—In English, those words that speak of possibility or necessity. I.E., can, can't, should.

Model of the World—A person's internal representation about the condition of the world.

Modeling—The NLP process of recreating excellence by isolating those elements necessary for excellent performance, and then replicating those elements in an easy-to-learn format.

MPVI™—Meta Programs and Values Inventory, a psychological profiling instrument which has the advantage of being able to be administered in an interview or on paper. The MPVI™ is available through Profitability Consulting.

Myers-Briggs—The Myers-Briggs Type Indicator is the most widely used psychological instrument in business and government today in profiling individuals as to personality.

NLP—Neuro Linguistic Programming. Neuro, refers to the mind and the nervous system through which the external sense impressions are received. Linguistic, refers to the language of the mind, including Visual, Auditory, Kinesthetic, Olfactory, Gustatory, and Auditory Digital.

Nominalization—Usually a verb or another process word which has been turned into a noun. The test for a nominalization is, "Can you put it into a wheelbarrow?"

Non-verbally—Without words. Usually referring to the analogue portion of our behavior such as tone of voice or other external behavior.

Part—A "part" of our personality, usually unconscious, which often has human attributes, which is responsible for maintaining a certain set of internal representations.

Perceiver—A preference in the Myers-Briggs category, Adaptation Response, Judger/Perceiver.

Phobia—A severe associated unwanted response of fear regarding some person or event in the past.

Reframe—Changing the context. Since all meaning is context dependent, by changing the context one can change the meaning of any word, or statement.

Representational System—A way of representing, internally, the external events that we perceive. There are six: Visual, Auditory, Kinesthetic, Olfactory, Gustatory, and Auditory Digital.

Sensor—A preference in the Myers-Briggs category, Internal State, Sensor/Intuitor

Sensory Acuity—Having very acute levels of sensory perception.

Sort—A computer term meaning to reorganize and/or to filter information in the process of that reorganization.

Submodality—A subset of or further distinctions of the modalities which are Visual, Auditory, Kinesthetic, Olfactory, Gustatory, and Auditory Digital. I.E., a submodality of visual would be the brightness of the picture.

Synesthesia—A pattern where two of the major representational systems are "hard wired" together over time, so that one follows the other in quick succession. E.G., "I want to see how I feel about that."

Time Line—The system for the organization of memories in the mind.

Toward—When a person's preference is to move in the direction of what they want.

Unconscious—The part of the mind which is not in our awareness, which is variously estimated to be in excess of 85%. The other than conscious, or subconscious.

Index